West Country
Edited by Claire Tupholme

 Young**Writers**

First published in Great Britain in 2006 by:
Young Writers
Remus House
Coltsfoot Drive
Peterborough
PE2 9JX
Telephone: 01733 890066
Website: www.youngwriters.co.uk

All Rights Reserved

© *Copyright Contributors 2006*

SB ISBN 1 84602 377 7

Foreword

This year, the Young Writers' *POP! - The Power Of Poetry* competition proudly presents a showcase of the best poetic talent selected from thousands of up-and-coming writers nationwide.

Young Writers was established in 1991 to promote the reading and writing of poetry within schools and to the young of today. Our books nurture and inspire confidence in the ability of young writers and provide a snapshot of poems written in schools and at home by budding poets of the future.

The thought, effort, imagination and hard work put into each poem impressed us all and the task of selecting poems was a difficult but nevertheless enjoyable experience.

We hope you are as pleased as we are with the final selection and that you and your family continue to be entertained with *POP! West Country* for many years to come.

Contents

Denmark Road High School for Girls, Gloucester
Olivia Ferguson (14)   1

Downfield Sixth Form, Stroud
Hannah Cleaver (16)   2
Christopher Julian Stanley (17)   3
Frances Forbes Carbines (16)   4
Meredith Fisk (16)   5

Hartcliffe Engineering College, Bristol
Jodie Mockridge (13)   5
Poppy Gates (12)   6
Sam Hughes (12)   6
Steph McCann (12)   7
Beau Baker (13)   7
Amy Ellery (12)   8
Jarrett Chamberlin (13)   8
Laura Davies (12)   9
Jack Painter (12)   9
Chelsey Taynton (13)   10
Georgina Dinham (12)   10
Terri Day (12)   11
Ben Lay (12)   11
Shellie Derrick (12)   12
Kesi Coombes (12)   12
Kayleigh Jordan Francis (12)   13
Lauren Hunt (12)   13
Chloe Perrott   14
Mitchell Player (12)   14
Luke Bishop (12)   15
Bobby Archard (12)   15
Luke Jones (13)   15
Michaela Vowles (12)   16
Zoë McAfee (12)   16
Emilene Davis (12)   17
Amy Dorney (12)   17
Sam Lovell (12)   18
Jack Moore (12)   18

Paige Willis (12)   18
Chloe Jayne Slater (12)   19
Scott Bush (12)   19
Jodie Bevan (13)   20
Alex Riddock (12)   21

King Edward's College, Bath
Connie Chapman (11)   21
Claire J Bowman (11)   22
Faye Maidment (11)   23
Sam Udale-Smith (11)   23
Hannah Pape (12)   24
Alex Prescot (11)   25
Freddie Knowlton (11)   26
Sam James Trapp (11)   26
Hannah Bostock (12)   27

Maidenhill School, Stonehouse
Oliver King (13)   28
Kelly Squibb (13)   29
Liam Neale (13)   30
Jemma Field (13)   31
Charlotte Davies (13)   32
Tayah Smith (13)   33
Deborah Sweetman (13)   33
Matthew Cole (13)   34
Hannah Herbert (14)   34
Naomi Gardener (13)   35
Nicolle Masson (13)   36
Camilla Woollard (13)   37
Zoe Barnes (14)   37
Sophie Organ (13)   38
Laura James (13)   39
Debra Bruton (13)   40
Casey Chandler (13)   41

Matravers School, Westbury
David Daniels (13)   41
Sian Plummer (13)   42
George Ward (13)   42

Jess Burry (13) 43
Chloe Carter 43
Callum Russell (13) 44
Aaron Lovelock (13) 44
Zoe Hyde (13) 45
James McDonald (14) 46

St Laurence School, Bradford-on-Avon
Heather Evans (11) 46
Rosie Pearce (12) 47
Eleanor Dodson (14) 48
Esther Jewitt (12) 49
James Lewis (11) 50

The Crypt School, Gloucester
Jacob McKenzie (11) 50
Henry Jordan (13) 51
Timothy Keasley (12) 52
Elias McGill (12) 52
Michael Philpott (11) 53
Liam Johnson (12) 53
Ieuan Prosser (11) 54
Callum Holder (11) 54
James Keasley (12) 55
Tom Thornes (12) 56
Jack Brickell (12) 57
Jack Woodward (11) 58
Simon Laird (15) 59
Trystan Archer (15) 60
Nicholas Walker (11) 61
Edward Kingston (11) 62
Ben Williams (11) 63
Russell Beacham (12) 64
Rupert Milward-Wiffen (12) 65

The Priory School, Taunton
Scott Gardner (14) 66
Joel Price (15) 66
Colin Walls (15) 67
Michael Harmer (15) 68

Thomas Keble School, Stroud

Georgia Watts (11)	68
Peter Moore (11)	68
Chelsea Hall (11)	69
Emma Jones (11)	69
Rebecca Fagg (11)	70
Fraser McLeod (11)	70
Hannah Rickards (11)	71
Liam Lines (11)	71
Nathan Piper (12)	71
Hayden Scamp (13)	72
Ellen Trueman (12)	72
Maizey Roberts (14)	73
Gracie Fickling (12)	73
Tim Coysh (12)	74
James Mahdiyone (12)	74
Sam Coxhead (11)	75
Kristina Peart (12)	75
Helena Short (14)	76
Liam Horsley (12)	76
Georgia Wood (12)	77
Lucy Wise (12)	77
Charlotte Granger (14)	78
Abi Wilkins & Fleur Tanner (12)	78
Tyrone Keene (14)	79
Jess Cox (12)	80
Finn Thomas-Cooney (11)	80
Amii Hughes (11)	81
Fay Hughes (12)	81
Charlotte Lane (11)	81
Liam Summers (11)	82
Eleanor Cairns (11)	82
Tom Carpenter (12)	82
Ashley Garraway (12)	83
Charlotte Watkins (14)	83
Stacey Cantillion (11)	83
Rhianne Banyard (14)	84
Amy Clark & Safaya Sutton (13)	85
Laura Wilkes (13)	86
Laura Bellamy (14)	87
John-Paul Crawford (12)	87
Johanna Barton (12)	88

Sophie Dewhurst (12)	88
Joshua Todd (13)	88
Matthew Austin (12)	89
Jordan Sowerby (13)	89
Alana Curtis (12)	89
Nicole Mallett (13)	90
Bille Marie Dimino (12)	90
Alice Gregory (11)	90
Amy Goldstone (12)	91
Megan Laws (12)	92
Angus McCrindle (12)	92
Catherine Marsden (14)	93
Adam Pinkney (12)	93
Ben Hassan (14)	94
Kenny Walker (12)	95
Joe Dickenson (13)	95
Gabriel Raeburn (14)	96
Rebecca Wallington (12)	96
Sam Nash (12)	97
Sam Evans (12)	97
Gemma Dianne Scrivens (14)	98
Jordan Frapwell (12)	98
Tadhg Martin-Haydock (14)	99
Timothy Williams (12)	99
Lisa Brown (12)	100
Oliver Jefferies (11)	100
Michael Paget (12)	101
Jonathon Sharp (11)	101
Bradley Sargent (11)	101
Gareth Frost (14)	102
Katie Stephens (11)	102
Lucy Stanford (14)	103
Nathan Huggins (11)	103
Isobel Percival (11)	104
Gemma Werrett (11)	104
Jemima Radmore (11)	104
Annie Hobbins (11)	105
Lara Crook (14)	105
Emma Freeman (14)	106
Clare Fickling (14)	106
Jessica Girdwood (11)	107
Josh Chambers (12)	107

Chris Lees (14)	108
Luke Cameron (11)	108
Stella Watts (15)	109
Josh Preece (11)	109
Sam Westerby (13)	110
Chris Evans (11)	110
Lizzie Warner (13)	111
Shauney Gobey (11)	111
Kelsey Ross (13)	112
Jack Gardiner (11)	112
Ben Dowdeswell (12)	113
Tom Woodward (12)	113
Oliver Bruce (12)	114
Sophie Townsend (11)	115
Molly Harris (11)	115
Michael Doolin (11)	116
Thomas Plaskitt (11)	116
Michael Hayward-Berry (15)	116
Jade Humphries (14)	117
Michael McClung (15)	117
Tyrell Edmond (14)	118
Luke Dyer (11)	118
Sam Reeves (14)	119
Guy Ridgway (11)	119
Cherrie-Jade Harrison (11)	120
Amy Bloomfield (13)	121
James Patrick McElroy (11)	121
Katharine Birkin (13)	122
Pete Morgan (14)	122
Katie Shaylor (13)	123
Kimberley Anne Cole (14)	123
Michael Ryan (14)	124
Ben Free (12)	125
Lisa Brazneill (14)	125
Rachel Bentall (15)	126
Rachel Montague (14)	126
Sophie Ryan (14)	127
Danie Russell (14)	127
Kerry Stephens (14)	128
Rachel Bedford (14)	129
Jemma Lewis (14)	130
Amanda Engstrom (13)	130

Megan Baker (13)	131
Isabelle Starkiss (13)	131
Rachel Rendell (15)	132
Sam Mincher (12)	132
Anika Ponting (12)	133
Nadine Marks (12)	133
Kayleigh Louise Adams (12)	134
Roberta Wilkes (12)	134
Paul Stephens (15)	135
Hannah Rachel Bucknell (12)	135
Ed Bryant (15)	136
Sophie Dennis (15)	137
Katie Ponting (15)	138
Becci Jennings (15)	138
Jamie Ponting (15)	139
Kate Melsome (16)	140
Robbie Gillett (15)	141
Kate Carpenter (15)	141
Sophie Jay Weston (12)	142
Hannah Wynter (12)	142
Annie Chaplin (12)	143
Liam Ballinger (12)	143
Miles Lewis-Iversen (12)	144
Rebecca Starkiss (15)	144
Billie Wiseman (12)	145
Jasmine Hicks (12)	145
Hannah Bloomfield (12)	146
Henry Walker (13)	146
Samuel Driscoll (13)	146
Craig Banyard (15)	147
Lisa Rice (15)	148
Josie Fowler (15)	149
Leah Pucknell (13)	150
Jordan Coxhead (13)	150
Perry Smith (12)	151
Emily McCollum (13)	151
Arthur Milroy (14)	152
Rosie Haighton (13)	152
Maya Schunemann (14)	153
Stephanie King (14)	153
Theo Deproost (15)	154
Jimmy Bower (14)	154

Andrew Roberts (14)	155
Lucy Cole (15)	155
Harley-Ray Hill (12)	156
Ben Jones (14)	156
Sam Sowerby (12)	157
Olivia Cole (13)	157
Adam Loveridge (14)	158
Christo Geller (14)	158
Tom Dunn (13)	159
Alistair Raghuram (14)	159
Jake Rogers (14)	160
Ryan Ponting (14)	161
Jay Newman (13)	161
Chris Whitfield (14)	162
Tom Organ (13)	162
Danielle Girdwood (14)	163
Emily Nobes (12)	163
Emma Townsend (14)	164
Alex Hunt (13)	164
Rowan Le Sage (14)	165
Kayleigh MacGillivray (15)	165
Harry Wilkins (15)	166
Joe Jenkins (14)	166
Tom Pugh (14)	167
Max Freedman (11)	167
Lauren Bown (14)	168
Amanda Gapp (13)	169
Sam Assanakis (13)	169
Corrie-Beth Hill (14)	170
Jade Shelton (13)	170

Westonbirt School, Tetbury

Victoria Butcher (11)	171
Alexia Kyriazi (11)	171
Georgina Lee (13)	172

The Poems

Dreaming, I Wonder

In dreaming, I wonder
Years from now
Will I be old?
Will I sit, an old woman
And consider what happened
To those dreams?
Those dreams I sent out,
Brave, lone boats
On a vast ocean.
Were they overcome?
When they vanished from my sight
Beyond the hopeful horizon
Were they flooded
And overwhelmed
By the great waves
That came to quash them?
Will I sit, an old woman
And never know what happened
To my dreams?
Dreaming, I wonder.

Olivia Ferguson (14)
Denmark Road High School for Girls, Gloucester

Above The Land

Way above land, in a place of freedom
Unbounded by rules, breaking all logic
Spontaneity unlike another
Surrounded by solitude

Thousands of ice-white droplets
Sunrises beyond imagination
Millions of companions
So distant from each other
Single, yet together

Storm of high intensity
Energy of life
Full of a hundred colours
Striking harshly
Onto deserted moors

Falling off the wing
Straight down below
Surrender to the hurricane
Let gravity take hold
Forget the pain

Stopped

By the abrupt change in pressure

Calm
Swiftly drift off the shore
Into the sunset
Just as it was before

Life in the air
Is so unreal
So unbelievably free
Understanding life
What we are meant to be.

Hannah Cleaver (16)
Downfield Sixth Form, Stroud

I Stabbed The Monarch
(But I Did Not Kill Macduff, The Swine)

Act II, Scene II

Duncan's dead
Stabbed in the bed
He bled and bled
My hands are red

I'll go to Hell
It won't be swell
The bell, the bell
Hope she won't tell

Act II, Scene III

Macduff is here
He's moved to tears
Then starts to jeer
I'm gripped with fear

Act III, Scene IV

I was his host
I see his ghost
He scares me most
In Hell I'll roast

Act V

My wife is dead
I'm filled with dread
Macduff sees red
I think I'm d . . .

Move along people, nothing to see here,
This is Middle-Age Scotland; it's a climate of fear . . .

Christopher Julian Stanley (17)
Downfield Sixth Form, Stroud

The Letter

He stands; a man bereft of hope,
His pallid face unfeeling
He sees the people come and go
He sees the never-ending flow
He sees, but no one comes and so,
His sad eyes trace the ceiling.

He thinks of when, back in his youth,
He stood at the same station
He'd waited long at platform four,
With thoughts of seeing her once more
He'd never burned like this before
Nor had this new sensation.

Her letter ran, 'I hope you'll see
That what you ask is madness
I've thought about it through and through
If I choose 'yes', I'll come to you
At Baker Street, our rendezvous,'
Reread the man with sadness.

With sinking heart he turns away
And heads towards his house
The letter from his pocket fell
A new excuse he'd have to tell
To those at home who loved him well;
His children and his spouse.

Frances Forbes Carbines (16)
Downfield Sixth Form, Stroud

Red Rose

A red rose blooms
The bud gently opening
Showing more of the red
It gets old and opens wide
Its petals falling to the ground

A red rose blooms
    Here on my wrist
The bud gently opening
    As the blood wells up
Showing more of the red
    My blood escaping
It gets old and opens wide
    The red stain spreading
The first petal falls
    Blood drips to the floor
It is all over for this little flower
    As I fall to the ground.

Meredith Fisk (16)
Downfield Sixth Form, Stroud

My Special Brother, Dan

Dan is my special brother
And there really is no other
He is a Bristol City fan
And he drinks Coke out of a can
And when the Bristol City win
He loves that more than anything
But when the Bristol City lose
He drowns his sorrow, jeers and boos
Through all the weather, wind and rain
He goes to see them, isn't that insane?
So do you think my brother is sad
I don't, I think he's Bristol City mad!

Jodie Mockridge (13)
Hartcliffe Engineering College, Bristol

Untitled

I was the one you left alone
I was the girl you locked in the closet
I was the boy who was never seen
I was the thing who was battered and bruised
I was the kid who was always hungry
I was the girl who couldn't speak
I was the boy who had no friends
I was the toy that never got played with
I was the book that was ripped and bent
I was the one whose heart you broke
I was the girl who was always alone
I was the teenager who was bullied
I was the boy who wore dirty clothes
I was the child who couldn't read and write
I was the girl with scruffy hair
I was the boy who couldn't play football
I was the girl who was ugly and spotty
I was the teenager on the streets
I was the old man who got mugged
I was the one who tried to kill myself.

Poppy Gates (12)
Hartcliffe Engineering College, Bristol

Sarah!

My sister, Sarah is Usher mad,
She writes everywhere, 'Usher's bad!'
She talks about him every day,
Sometimes, I wish she'd go away.
As big sisters go, I suppose she's all right,
But she does my head in, when she talks all night!
She listens to music rather a lot,
Her friends in school all call her Dot!
But if she wasn't here, I'd really miss
Having her as *my big sis!*

Sam Hughes (12)
Hartcliffe Engineering College, Bristol

Untitled

I was the child you left alone
I was the toddler you punched and hit
I was the teenager who you threw in the pit
I was the youth you beat to the ground
I was the toddler you were kicking around
I was the adult beaten at home
I was the teenager left in the dark alone
I live in silence, I live in the dark
I was the child who was hit with your flying dart
I was the person who was unloved
I look up at the sky wondering if God would help me up above
I was the boy who waited and waited
I was the girl that was beaten and hated
On the day that I was born
My heart was broken
I was the baby who awoke
I was the girl you pinched and poked
I was the thing you strangled with lace
I was the person who put on a brave face.

Steph McCann (12)
Hartcliffe Engineering College, Bristol

My 13th Autumn

I'm becoming aware
Of all the things autumn has to share
Heaps full of fun
Heaps full of leaves
All of them falling from the trees.
Burning fires come at last
Reminds me of autumns from the past
I look out of my window
I sit there and gaze
A typical view of an autumn haze.

Beau Baker (13)
Hartcliffe Engineering College, Bristol

I Was The Child

I was the child who was left alone
I was the niece you threw in the garden
I was the baby you beat to the ground
I was the boy you despised
I was the eye that saw everything
I was the baby who was abandoned because you were too young
I was the ear that had to listen to you
I was the body that had no clothes
I was the person who hated myself
I was the granddaughter whose heart you broke inside
I was the cat that nearly got killed
I was the daughter who had no clothes
I was the cousin that wasn't loved
I was the girl who was bullied because I was ugly with hair not brushed
 I was the sister you thought was invisible
I was the glass that was picked up and stuck in someone's arm
I was the brother who wasn't applauded or honoured
I was the innocent one who was blamed for everything
I was a somebody who thought was a nobody
I was the one that was treated like dirt.

Amy Ellery (12)
Hartcliffe Engineering College, Bristol

Firework Fun

The green leaves turning as gold as the sun,
The autumn air cutting into our thick skin,
Everybody's outside raking the leaves, having fun,
Spinning about in their little silver tins,
People collecting conkers, but where am I?
'Chop, chop, Charlie! We're leaving!' I hear my mum scream,
So I really must go, must see the firework show!

Jarrett Chamberlin (13)
Hartcliffe Engineering College, Bristol

My Dad, Glenn

My dad is married, to my mum
Who she thinks has a brilliant bum
My dad is nice with a rounded belly
Although his feet can be rather smelly
He has short hair upon his head
But not as short as Right Said Fred
He loves to watch the footie on the telly
While resting a beer upon his belly
He has ten fingers and ten toes
And lots of freckles on his nose
His knobbly knees, they knock together
Abut I don't care, so whatever
My mum says he snores in bed
And that he's done so since they wed
He's 41 and getting old
One good thing is, that he's not bald
He may still have a few spots
But I still love him, lots and lots!

Laura Davies (12)
Hartcliffe Engineering College, Bristol

The Season Is Coming

The night starts to get dark early,
The leaves are changing colour,
Hallowe'en costumes start to sell
And the leaves start to fall.
The fireworks are ready,
The parties are just beginning,
You can hear the conkers fall,
You and your friends jump in the leaves,
For the big season is coming.
It's autumn!

Jack Painter (12)
Hartcliffe Engineering College, Bristol

Autumn Days . . .

Autumn days
We sit and gaze
At all the things outside

Leaves are blowing
It's not snowing
But it's still quite cold outside

Hallowe'en what joy it brings
Sweets and dressing up
Bonfire Night, Bonfire Night
Sparklers and fireworks are all in sight

But when it's time for autumn
Leaves are everywhere
Orange ones and bronze ones
All blowing in the air

Jumping in the leaves
What joy it has to bring
Autumn days
We sit and gaze
At all the wonderful things.

Chelsey Taynton (13)
Hartcliffe Engineering College, Bristol

Autumn Poem

Leaves are falling
Autumn calling
Winter on its way.
Bonfire's burning,
Red, blue and grey.

Georgina Dinham (12)
Hartcliffe Engineering College, Bristol

Devastation!

First the Twin Towers,
Then the bus and the train,
Bang! Go the terrorists, again and again.

All those innocent people,
Only passing through,
No one expected it, not me or you.

It was a terrible scene,
With victims so sad,
Those days we'll remember, we should never have had.

Fire crews and paramedics,
The police turned up too,
They were all so shocked, they didn't know what to do.

They fought so hard,
Those days in vain,
We all prayed to God, this would never happen again.

And all of us know,
The terrorists are still about,
But we have to live with this, day in, day out.

Terri Day (12)
Hartcliffe Engineering College, Bristol

Autumn

Autumn's the best
It's better than the rest
Crashing and banging
Sparkling and glowing.

One, two, three, the fireworks are in the air
If you stand really close
You will get blown up
Into the air.

Ben Lay (12)
Hartcliffe Engineering College, Bristol

Bump In The Night

I lie in my bed ready to sleep
Awaiting the dreaded alarm clock beep
I'm falling asleep upon my bunk
Then woken by the boiler, *clunk!*

I lie in my bed ready to sleep
Awaiting the dreaded alarm clock beep
I'm dozing off, about to sleep
Then woken by the floorboard creak.

I lie in my bed ready to sleep
Awaiting the dreaded alarm clock beep
Comfortably led, relaxing quick
Then woken by the thermostat click.

I lie in my bed ready to sleep
Awaiting the dreaded alarm clock beep
My eyes are dropping, as warm as a chick
Then woken by the copper pipe click.

I lie in my bed ready for sleep
Awaiting the dreaded alarm clock beep
Finally, in a deep, deep sleep
Then woken by the *alarm clock beep!*

Shellie Derrick (12)
Hartcliffe Engineering College, Bristol

Autumn

Leaves the colour of fire,
Fireworks exploding,
Pumpkins glowing warmly in windows,
Weather getting colder,
Children out, it's Hallowe'en,
Leaves falling from the trees,
Small children collecting conkers.

Kesi Coombes (12)
Hartcliffe Engineering College, Bristol

Fairies

Fairies flying about the night,
Only one little boy can see them in sight!

They're wearing dresses like fairies do
And every night the boy asks, 'Who are you?'

He stops and stares in his garden,
The fairies whisper and he says, 'Pardon?'

This boy, he's only seven,
But asks if they come from Heaven.

His name is Little Jack,
He wonders why the fairies have wings on their back.

They fly about every night and day,
Wondering if Jack will ever play.

Jack tells him mum, she thinks he's mad,
But she thinks about it . . . fairies wouldn't be so bad!

Jack was in the garden, playing all day,
He played with the fairies and they took him away!

Kayleigh Jordan Francis (12)
Hartcliffe Engineering College, Bristol

Looking

The autumn season is coming near,
As fireworks shoot in the air,
Boom! Bang! Crackle!
A wonderful sound of cheer,
Soon, there will be pumpkins
And trick or treaters more,
To make us laugh and giggle,
As the nights come here and there,
But nobody seems to realise,
There's more than just the fun,
There is just looking and looking and looking,
At the colours of the season's *beauty!*

Lauren Hunt (12)
Hartcliffe Engineering College, Bristol

The Globe

Why are we polluting
When we could be diluting?
Earthquakes appear
And hurricanes each year.
Tsunamis and gales
Bring terrible tales
Of damage and death
And fighting for breath,
With pure, clean air
So drastically rare.
There's a solution
To this type of pollution.
Things will get worse
In this great universe
Unless it's seen
We intend to go green
And stick to the letter,
To make things a lot better.

Chloe Perrott
Hartcliffe Engineering College, Bristol

My Brother

My brother, my brother
He talks like my mother,
We're always arguing with one another,
He kicks and screams until he gets his own way,
On the occasional day,
I understand my brother's demands,
But if he goes ballistic,
I remember my brother Kieran,
Is autistic.

Mitchell Player (12)
Hartcliffe Engineering College, Bristol

The Fun Of Autumn

The pile of leaves are like a bush on fire,
The night creeps in early,
Booms, bangs and *screeches,*
Fireworks, sparklers and a bonfire, as warm as a volcano,
Hallowe'en has passed, with me having no fun,
I won't be collecting conkers,
Cracking the marvellous shell,
Because I have a cold.

Luke Bishop (12)
Hartcliffe Engineering College, Bristol

Oblivion

Every day we are getting older,
Each day we are becoming bolder,
But do we think twice about our fate,
We never hardly think about our set date,
Maybe it's tomorrow or fifty years,
But for most common people this is the least of our fears,
As we wreck our home,
Our Earth,
What will there be for the next generation,
At birth?

Bobby Archard (12)
Hartcliffe Engineering College, Bristol

Autumn

I was walking along the pavement
The rustle of the dead leaves flew past me
As cars went zooming past.

Then I hear a *swoosh*
And I am stood soaked from a puddle
And covered in wet leaves.

Luke Jones (13)
Hartcliffe Engineering College, Bristol

On The Way Home

Squish, squash, splatter!
As my foot hit the mud
The rattle of the rain splashing heavily
The brown, crispy leaves are crunching
As I plod on home.

Every step I take, I can see less behind me
Because the mist covers it up
The cold, wet wind is coming against me
As I jump the rushing streams.

Finally, I come to my house
Take off the sopping wet clothes
Change into my nice, warm PJs
And sit by the hot, cosy fire.

Michaela Vowles (12)
Hartcliffe Engineering College, Bristol

A Friend

Someone to comfort,
To dry your tears.

Someone to be there,
To quieten your fears.

A companion, a pal,
A very best friend.

Someone to trust
And love till the end.

You are always there
When I need you.

Devoted, loving and true,
No one could wish for anything more.

Than a faithful friend like you!

Zoë McAfee (12)
Hartcliffe Engineering College, Bristol

Autumn

Autumn is cold and cloudy,
Conkers fall to the ground,
Cuddling up to your cuddly bear,
In front of the crackling fire.

The grass chattered when the frost settled,
Trees laughed when they saw themselves bare
And the rest of the park laughed with them,
The pavement of the park cried with fear
As the trick or treaters ran over it,
Leaves giggled as they wriggled to the ground,
The wind whispered in the night,
The wolves howled to the sound.

It was the darkest night in autumn
And I was walking home, when *boom!*
There was a beautiful firework display,
Then there was the *sizzle* of the sizzling, sparkling sparklers.

Emilene Davis (12)
Hartcliffe Engineering College, Bristol

Autumn

In autumn, in the freezing cold,
With the soggy mud sticking to my shoes,
I like to splash about
In my big, puffy coat,
With the bang of the fireworks
And the explosions in the air!

Snow is never in the summer
It's always white and cold
But if the sun and snow's together
All that falls is never gold.

The trickling sound of the snowflakes falling
And the sound of the water coming,
With the light blue sky and the light blue clouds
That everyone is loving!

Amy Dorney (12)
Hartcliffe Engineering College, Bristol

Autumn

The leaves swish side to side,
You can hear the crunching of the leaves as you walk,
The leaves change colour through the autumn,
Wind blows the trees, that makes the leaves fall to the ground,
Trees make a new beginning,
That's why autumn is just amazing,
Hallowe'en is scary for small kids, but fun for big kids,
People get sweets by knocking on doors
And saying, 'Happy Hallowe'en!'

Sam Lovell (12)
Hartcliffe Engineering College, Bristol

Autumn

As I walked into my house,
The roar of the fire hit me,
The cry of the wind
And the shake of the trees,
Rattled all night long.

In the morning they fell,
As if it were in slow motion,
I opened my door as it screamed
And the rush of cold air struck me!

Jack Moore (12)
Hartcliffe Engineering College, Bristol

Autumn

Fireworks screamed as they hit off into the dark, cold sky,
Sparklers sizzling as they fly off deep in the sky,
Spinners shouting stop as freezing cold rain hits their sides,
The night is coming to an end,
At least the fireworks had a good time,
Flying through the air!

Paige Willis (12)
Hartcliffe Engineering College, Bristol

Untitled

In the autumn, in the freezing cold,
With the soggy mud, I like to splash about in my coat
With the crisp of the leaves
And the splodge of the mud.

Leaves go crispy and the cold air goes clear
When the weather goes white and the grass goes glazey,
When weather is cold and cloudy
And conkers fall to the ground.

Leaves go blue as frost touches,
The puddles frown as they go all icy,
The sky is happy as Jack Frost comes,
With all the kids and mums,
All the buildings frown as they all close down,
As all the grown-ups do Christmas shopping in town.

All the witches and ghosts come out at night,
Giving all the girls and boys a fright!

Chloe Jayne Slater (12)
Hartcliffe Engineering College, Bristol

What Is The Cold?

The cold of autumn is like a cloudy sky in the night
The cold is like the coughing of a man
The cold is like a cold cat as it crunches crinkly leaves
The cold is like conkers
The cold is like a kid's head in the clouds
The clouds are very white in the cold
The cold is like a kid kicking conkers
The cold is like a screaming kid in the cold, cold snow
The cold is like feet crunching crinkly leaves.

Scott Bush (12)
Hartcliffe Engineering College, Bristol

A Day Of School

Children pushing, teachers shushing,
Names are listing, tongue twisting,
Pupils learning, minds are turning,
That's one lesson done.

Get ready, set, go under water, bubbles flow
Swimming fast and swimming slow
The water ripples down below,
That's two lessons done.

Bell's buzzing, people rushing just to get a snack,
Vending lending, buying, *mmm* satisfying
Ring, ring! Bell's gone better get to class,
But see what lesson we have next, it's maths.

First of all, six times table, go up to ten if you're able,
Now get your maths books and turn to page twenty
Have a look, there's sure to be plenty,
That's three lessons done.

Test tubes and Bunsen burners,
Don't mess about, there's a lot to learn,
Bags under tables, stools tucked in,
We must be safe before we begin,
That's four lessons done.

Cards out to get some lunch,
What can I have for my afternoon munch?
I get my meal and water from a spring,
Just as I finished, the bell went *ring!*

This lesson's a double session of art, we're crafting things
Like a cardboard house, plastic mice
And birds that have long wings.

Now it's the end of the day,
I'm going to go home,
Get changed and play!

Jodie Bevan (13)
Hartcliffe Engineering College, Bristol

Dragon Soul

A dragon's soul is very clever,
A dragon's soul is there forever and ever,
When a dragon dies it disappears,
Washing away all its fears,
A dragon's soul goes to a special place,
Somewhere up there, in outer space,
If a dragon's soul isn't allowed in this place
It is vanquished to Hell,
Where it lies motionless with no other use,
But to reckon with its wrong doings,
A dragon's soul is very clever!

Alex Riddock (12)
Hartcliffe Engineering College, Bristol

Witch Dance

The witches are dancing
Around the open fire,
Their awful looks and creepy chants
Make me feel quite dire.

Dare I creep a little nearer?
I don't know if I should,
Everything is going wrong
In the darkened wood.

The cold and dark is drawing in,
I'm beginning to feel quite scared,
If they come and sniff me out,
I won't be well prepared.

The witches have finished their creepy chant,
They've raised a skinny finger,
It's pointed right at the place I hide,
I don't think I should linger.

Connie Chapman (11)
King Edward's College, Bath

The Devil Adder

The ebony night,
Advancing on me,
As I spied through the charms,
A malevolent tree.

An adder I spied,
In the bay of the keep,
With its slippery scales,
I thought it asleep.

I pondered awhile,
Then walked up to the snake,
Then it *struck!* and vanished,
I couldn't help but shake.

The whispering venom,
In my trembling leg,
Then a rustle, and
I smelt a poached egg.

It was but a dream,
In my poor head,
For hunger struck me,
Was I dead?

I was falling,
Through a deep, black red,
It was blood
And I was filled with dread.

My shock was deadly,
When the fire appeared,
One more second of life?
Then the Devil, he jeered.

Claire J Bowman (11)
King Edward's College, Bath

The Witch

The fearful witch, the fearless witch,
Without the slightest noise,
Waits cautiously outside a school,
To feast on girls and boys.

She carefully opens up her bag,
Full of sweets and treats,
She applies her gloves, make-up and more
Then cackles at the mischief she's got in store!

The school clock strikes four, it's time to go home,
But what happens to the children is unknown,
For we must depart and not be seen,
Or we will be turned into slime green,
Because the witches' brew and witches' stew
I wouldn't go out if I were you!

Faye Maidment (11)
King Edward's College, Bath

The Haunted Mansion

Down in the haunted mansion
At the end of the cobbled street
Where the pictures watch you
And evil doesn't sleep

I checked my wizard spellbook
And crept down one dark night
For I could summon forth to me
An army full of might

Army of darkness
I summon you
We shall all fight
Evil things we can do.

Sam Udale-Smith (11)
King Edward's College, Bath

The Dance On Hallows Eve

On a desolate landscape,
In a forest of green,
There are ghoulies and ghosties,
Huddling unseen,
In wait for the waltz,
For the dance to begin,
For the harps to strike up
And the night to fall in,
Make haste, make haste,
For you don't want to be
Outside a warm home
On All Hallows Eve.
The clock strikes its twelve,
But the sound won't be heard,
As the song has begun
And you can't say a word,
As they'll cut you and rip you,
Chew you and bite you,
You wouldn't escape,
They would eat you and hide you,
On All Hallows Eve,
They dance till morn's high,
Then they hide until next time,
When night is on high.

Hannah Pape (12)
King Edward's College, Bath

The Memory Charm

Into the gloomy forest I crept,
Into the darkening abyss I stepped,
Through engulfing quicksand and ebony black,
Until I came to the disused shack.

I heard some voices, high-pitched and cold,
Very sinister and very bold,
Muttering a language unlike mine
And on a fire a cauldron did shine.

Into the cauldron they put a frog,
A bat, a cat and a repulsive dog,
An elephant's tusk, a bony bird
And then came the malevolent voice I heard.

'The final ingredient for my charm,
Is a boy of twelve's little arm,
It must have fat, not skin and bone,
I need it now!' she did moan.

At this, I felt a shiver of cold,
One of the witches, perhaps the most old,
Had seen me, with a cry of delight,
'We will get the arm tonight!'

I ran and ran and ran some more,
I ran until my feet were sore,
Out of the forest and into my room,
I had just escaped my doom!

Alex Prescot (11)
King Edward's College, Bath

A Spell For Reincarnation

A witch on a desolate hill,
Mumbling and jumbling words from a spell.
'Bats, lizards, frogs, toads, snakes, ravens, spiders,
Come to me so I can see your presence,
My spell will be complete with you in my cauldron.'

'My cat, please come to me, bring the body of Ravenal Hell,
My cat come on my broomstick,
Come to where my ancestors used to live.'

'The skies of evil hear my spell,
Jet-black cauldron rise to the sky,
Bring back the soul of Ravenal Hell,
Come down to me and I will take you back on my broomstick.'

She cackled all the way back until she lost her voice,
The only thing she did forget,
Was she didn't close the door to Hell.

Freddie Knowlton (11)
King Edward's College, Bath

The Ebony Witches

Malevolent ingredients they added today,
Gruesome, gruesome, you would say,
Smell as bad as sausage and peach,
Mixed with repulsive sand from the beach.
Frog leg, mince pies and banana split
And goat horn that went off with a hit,
Horse nose, cow leg and salty snails,
Smelly manure, cat ear and cricket bails.
Pickled eggs mixed with Cheddar cheese,
Covered by golden leaves flying in the breeze,
Disgusting, disgusting, it will make you feel ill,
The gruesome contents into the fill,
It may seem gruesome to you and me,
But the ebony witches eat it for tea.

Sam James Trapp (11)
King Edward's College, Bath

Wanted - A Barn Owl

I'm looking for a barn owl,
Must be full of spite.
A smallish size,
But full of might.
Be an expert at screeching
And good in a flight.

I'm looking for a barn owl,
To fly for me at night.
Must have big eyes to be my cautious spy,
An ebony owl to hide at night
And be adept,
At scanning the skies.

I'm looking for a barn owl,
With a great, hot temper.
A knowledge of spells
And a sly smile.
One with strong nerves,
The salary's high.

I'm looking for a barn owl,
Only the best need apply.

Hannah Bostock (12)
King Edward's College, Bath

Ode To A Wrapped Sweet

My tiny chocolate cuboid lays waiting on a desk,
Wrapped in a blue, starry, shiny wrapper,
Teasing me, pulling me ever closer,
With its curious colours and shapes.

My tiny sweet, as I smelt it, I sense the Galaxy, milky chocolate,
Which is imprisoned in plastic wrapping,
As if it's suffocating in a brittle tin of bendy,
Stretchy, crisp material.

When I put my tiny present of packaging to my ear,
I can hear the rustling, like a tiny mouse
Bursting Rice Crispies.
Pop! Crackle! Burst!

As I run my finger over my little sensation,
I feel a smooth, lumpy texture with sharp, pointing wings,
Waiting to be unwrapped by my giant fingers.

As I put my small sensation in my mouth, it gives me satisfaction,
As I wrap my tongue around the creamy chocolate, melting it away
And stick the remaining soft, chewy nougat
Between my teeth and quickly devour it.

Oliver King (13)
Maidenhill School, Stonehouse

Boyz!

Boyz mess with your head,
Boyz mess with your mind,
You may think they're sweet,
You may think they're kind!

They're all the same,
They all tell lies,
Some wear suits,
Some wear ties!

They tell you they love you,
That's just a joke,
Some boyz drink,
Others smoke!

'I'll always be with you,'
They say aloud,
Even though it's a lie,
They say it so proud!

'Why can't they change?'
Us girls say, madly,
We need them to change,
Us girls want it badly!

Yes, boyz are fit,
Yes, boyz are fine,
Yes, we love them,
Because they're so divine!

So, next time, when you think you've found the one,
Hold him tight and don't let him run!

Kelly Squibb (13)
Maidenhill School, Stonehouse

Halo 2 Poem

Please let me have five minutes of fame,
As Halo 2 is my favourite game.
Master Chief against the flood
And covenants all immersed in blood.
Sniping ghosts from hilltops high,
Making young Americans cry.
Running riot with an energy sword,
Playing rumble pit when you're totally bored.
Capturing the flag on Burial Mound,
Sneaking in the base without a sound.
Plasma grenades and melee attacks,
Picking up ammo and medical packs.
At 5am you still feel the tension,
Playing rocket ball on maps, like Ascension.
Warthogs and ghosts on Coagulation.
Playing Halo 2 such a gaming sensation.
Spectres are cool makes Halo so great,
Mowing people down is a piece of cake.
Campaign mode is absolutely ace,
With glitches all around the place.
Vehicles are good when they're nice and fresh,
But watch out for fences of wire mesh.
Xbox live makes you want to rule the land,
But don't cheat or you will get banned.
My gamer tag is *'Slasher Strike'*,
If you think you can beat me, take a hike!
So here I am, at the end of this poem,
I guess I'd better say bye and get going.
Halo 2 is my favourite game,
So let me have five minutes of fame!

Liam Neale (13)
Maidenhill School, Stonehouse

How Is That Hanging Up There?

How is that hanging up there?
How is that hanging up there?
There is an eagle that stares,
Close my mind,
Close the door,
You won't see me anymore.

A baby that cries,
Deserves to survive,
In this cold world,
I call mine.

Mice scuttle around my feet,
Under sofas going *squeak, squeak,*
Cats on the patrol
Waiting to pounce
On the prize.

People waiting silently,
Queuing for hope or joy,
Close my mind,
Close the door,
You won't see me anymore.

Jemma Field (13)
Maidenhill School, Stonehouse

Ode To A Wrapped Sweet

He sits there, a man left outside,
In the miserable, moaning rain and wind,
He sits on the step, wrapped in his purple glistening coat.

He slowly, smoothly, gradually gets up,
But feels stiff, like a twig just fallen from its tree,
His sparkling coat sounds like tiny feet stamping,
In a puddle but not calm rain,
The autumn leaves crunch in my mind I hear the coat rustle.

He sits outside a chocolate shop,
The magical smell got lost in the winter's breeze,
The sweet aroma follows him through
The winding streets chasing him like a shadow.

He takes his glistening coat from around him,
Sharp, but melting shoulders his cube-like body wanders
Around, slipping and sliding in and out of puddles until *splash!*
He fails into a melting burst of taste but suddenly
Something lifts him up to a black hole high above him.

He feels piercing pain like knives stabbing,
Through his solid, silk, irresistible, soaked body,
His glistening coat is now lost into the mystic memories
He relaxes as he sails down a black hole
And plummets into my Dairy Milk stream.

Charlotte Davies (13)
Maidenhill School, Stonehouse

Love

Your heart left pumping
In and out,
You know it's love
Without a doubt.

Roses, chocolates
The whole works,
The butterfly moments,
It has its quirks.

A candlelit dinner
A romantic night,
Your guest stood waiting,
Oh, what a sight!

Your heart left pumping
In and out,
You know it's love,
Without a doubt!

Tayah Smith (13)
Maidenhill School, Stonehouse

One Night In October

For one night only in October,
People buy sweets
And carve out pumpkins.
Children dress up in scary costumes,
Then knock on doors
And say 'trick or treat'.
They will get sweets
And do this to every house in their street.
Then go back home
And enjoy their treats.
This all happens on the 31st
And is called Hallowe'en!

Deborah Sweetman (13)
Maidenhill School, Stonehouse

Movies

They're to entertain,
To make you laugh,
Or scare you.

Action,
Sci-fi,
Whatever you're into.

Take anyone,
You'll have people who hate it,
People who love it, people who laughed
And people who didn't get it.

Sequels,
Chronicles,
They're to entertain,
Movies are cool.

Matthew Cole (13)
Maidenhill School, Stonehouse

Autumn

In autumn the leaves fall down
Golden, crispy and brown
Walking in them, make a crunch
I like to scoop up a bunch.

Then I throw them in the air
Some people stop to stare
As the leaves land in my hair
But I don't give a care.

The berries are red and bright
Green leaves disappeared from sight
The frost will soon be all around
Even snow may be on the ground.

Hannah Herbert (14)
Maidenhill School, Stonehouse

Ying And Yang

Big elephant
Small mouse
Different sizes
But can live in harmony

Icy cold
Summer warm
Two different temperatures
Same type of thing

Lion fierce
Kitten soft
Two cats
Different personalities

Hero good
Villain evil
Superhero people
Changing lives in different ways

Sunny sky
Grassy earth
Flying high in the air
Lying low on the floor

Pitch-black
Glowing white
Both colours of darkness and light
Both colours get on well

All these things
Not the same
But so alike
Because without them
Where would we be?

Naomi Gardener (13)
Maidenhill School, Stonehouse

Teenage Life

Parents get on your nerves,
They just don't understand,
Life is so confusing,
When you're a teenager in demand.

Beauty products and hair dye,
Losses of boyfriends
That makes you cry.

MP3s and mobile phones,
All sassy and stylish,
You got all the latest tunes and tones,
Just like your friends wish.

New style and shades,
What should I show off on,
Bike, scooter or blades?

No more toys for Christmas,
What you gonna choose?
Not that long till you're 18,
Then you can ask for booze.

Birthday's coming up soon,
Not much longer to wait,
The school dance is coming soon too,
I hope I get a date.

Teenage spots are breaking out,
Where is that concealer?
It works like a gem,
But the spot cream's the real healer.

Smoking, sex and drugs
And teenage cracks,
That's what boys look for,
But girls focus on their beauty packs.

Nicolle Masson (13)
Maidenhill School, Stonehouse

Christmas Is Coming!

Christmas is coming
I love this time of year
Everybody's happy
And full of good cheer.

I'm going to build a snowman
He brings me so much fun
With his black coal eyes and carrot nose
And a smile for everyone.

It won't be long now, it comes round very quick
For his reindeer and Sir Nick
When the reindeer land on the roof
You hear the prancing of each little hoof
It puts a smile on my face
And warns me with much grace.

I am so excited to see what he has left
But I'd better go to sleep maybe for the best
But I fall asleep, snuggled in my bed
With weird and wonderful dreams whirling in my head!

Camilla Woollard (13)
Maidenhill School, Stonehouse

Poem About Terrorism

Terrorism, terrorism, isn't very civilism
Planning things,
Plotting things,
I don't like the pain it brings.
Many lives have been lost,
What a cost, what a cost!
The innocent are brought to tears,
The young are forced into fears.
I wish that we could catch them,
The ones that bring the mayhem.

Zoe Barnes (14)
Maidenhill School, Stonehouse

Myths And Legends

A dragon, a unicorn,
A fairy or two,
A wizard, a witch,
A monkey doing kung fu!

These are all myths,
Some are legends,
On whether you believe,
It all depends.

I believe,
So I have,
Seen a dragon,
Rode a unicorn,
Said a spell with a wizard,
Rode a broom with a witch
And had kung fu lessons with a monkey!

If you want to do,
What I have done,
Then believe in what you hear
And let your imagination run.

So don't forget,
If you think you're alone,
There are friends in your mind,
Waiting for the chance to roam.

Around your life there they'll be,
Waiting for you to return,
To pick up your pen
And draw them again,
So that once again they may be,
As lively as a kangaroo
And as free as a bee!

Sophie Organ (13)
Maidenhill School, Stonehouse

My Family

My family is special
They are always there
Sometimes Mum and Dad
But mostly my brother

Martyn is my brother
But he gets called Spud
He's 17 years old
Protective over me

My dad works at Woodlodge
Delivering plant pots
Earning lots of money
By working quite a lot

My mum works at Golden Valley
Filling vending machines
She works for my uncle
And his partner too

My brother's doing an apprenticeship
Training in carpentry
He's doing it at Stroud College
Two days a week

I've got close to my nanna James
Since my grandad died
We never used to see her much
We never had the time
And now my nanna comes to stay
Nearly all the time

I have many cousins
But I'm only close to two
We spend a lot of time together
Laughing through and through.

Laura James (13)
Maidenhill School, Stonehouse

Ode To A Wrapped Sweet

The lifeless, idle, camouflage chocolate Snickers,
With big, blue, beady eyes.
Just perching there longing to be devoured,
As in crow configuration,
It screeches out over schedules,
To be devoured.

It, the crow, who has a caramel fragrance,
Smothered in a nutty sensation.
Just perching there longing to be devoured,
As in crow configuration,
It screeches out over schedules,
To be devoured.

It's rustic, standing on leaves sound,
Begins to be preyed on by the next-door neighbour's cat,
Its tight leaves begin to become sweaty overtime.
Just perching there longing to be devoured,
As in crow configuration,
It screeches out over schedules,
To be devoured.

To be as hard as a blackboard, screeching when written on,
As its rustic ways and bracings make it have a train touch.
Just perching there longing to be devoured,
As in crow configuration,
It screeches out over schedules,
To be devoured.

His beady eyes,
Always surrounded by a soothing, soft, sensuous heart.
Just perching there longing to be devoured,
As in crow configuration,
It screeches out over schedules,
To be devoured.

Debra Bruton (13)
Maidenhill School, Stonehouse

Friendship

Friends are important to me
Especially Laura and Zoe
They're always there when I'm upset
They're so important to me

I don't know what I'd do without them
No one to talk to, tell my secrets, or text on my phone
I'd be very lonely without them
They're so important to me

Me and Laura met in Year 7
And we will always be mates no matter what
Me and Zoe met in Reception
And will be mates and never forget

That's why I'm writing this poem to tell you how cool they are
How much they mean to me
What would I do without them?
Hope we stay forever friends, forever!

Casey Chandler (13)
Maidenhill School, Stonehouse

The Mummy

Carried from the black lands
Supported but alone
To the red lands for my burial

Tightly embalmed in a linen sheet
Surrounded by a silver canopy of spider webs
Anubis and Horus accompany me
On the journey to the Field of Reeds

Slowly, slowly,
As my bones crumble
Into the ground
I listen to the silence
And wait.

David Daniels (13)
Matravers School, Westbury

The Mummy

Here I am,
Sleeping still,
In a dark, dusty, cold tomb,
My canopic jars beside me,
A canopy of cobwebs,
Draped above my final resting place.

I've left the world of wearing linen and cloth,
Now I lie here naked and brown,
Around me, murals of Egyptians and hieroglyphics,
My tired bones cracking as time goes on.

Anubis stares at me from the darkness,
Guardian of my forgotten tomb,
Head of the jackal,
His mask worn by priests,
Who left me here alone,
Waiting to meet my ancestors.

Sian Plummer (13)
Matravers School, Westbury

Into The Darkness

Carried from the flooded plains of the Nile
From black land to the red lands
Dreaming of the Field of Reeds

Buried with my mortal possessions
Curled to face the east
My knees drawn up against my chin
My skin tightening, shrivelling back
Into a thousand-year-old baby

Against the feather of truth lies my heart
I wait to bribe the gatekeepers
And enter the kingdom of Osiris
But still I wait, turning into dust
As I travel out of the light
And into the darkness.

George Ward (13)
Matravers School, Westbury

The Mummy

Taken by torch light down the cold, sandy steps,
I'm all on my own now,
Tired and scared.

There are jars around me which contain my insides,
My belongings beside me,
I face east, waiting to be reborn.

Embalmed in a linen shroud,
Surrounded by darkness and death,
Insects scuttle over my broken bones.

I am in my coffin, so cold, dark and empty,
My tomb is covered in spiders' webs,
The walls around me full of hieroglyphics.

My hair slowly shrivelling,
My bones begin to crack,
My skin taught and torn.

Dreaming of my rebirth,
Waiting for reunion with Osiris,
In the Fields of Reeds.

Jess Burry (13)
Matravers School, Westbury

Not The Furniture Game

His hair was a static shock,
His eyes were a bullet in the chest,
His clothes were a funeral.
His jokes were a punch in the arm,
His laugh was a frog in the rain.
His skin was the surface of the moon,
His mood was an angry dog.

His wife was a spinning top
And she disappeared,
Like the blue sky.

Chloe Carter
Matravers School, Westbury

The Mummy

I am carried from the rich banks of the Nile
In a long procession
Accompanied by the chanting of priests
To the blazing, burning desert.
The juice is squeezed from me
My possession buried, but faded.

Here I lie crippled and cracked
In the piercing, pitch-black tomb
My innards lie all around me.

I choke on the murky air, cough
I've been tampered with
All I have looking over me are my gods.

Waiting for Anubis to measure my worth
At the gates to the Field of Reeds.

Callum Russell (13)
Matravers School, Westbury

The Mummy

My ba, my ka, have disappeared
Akh has flown to the stars
My dirty body wrapped in cloth
My cold tomb surrounds me
My organs cold in pretty jars
My insides empty and cold.

I have jewels to slick the hand
Which holds the key to my freedom
The Field of Reeds is but a dream
One that will never come true
So I lie here waiting
Nothing but rotting cloth.

Aaron Lovelock (13)
Matravers School, Westbury

The Mummy

Here I lie, deep, dark and alone
Under a tower of brick and stone
I stare into the murky gloom
Golden figures surround my tomb

In my sarcophagus I lie
How I wish I could see the sky
Waiting for Thoth, my judge and my scribe
Surrounded by jewels, the gatekeepers bribe

My organs beside me in canopic jars
Already I've travelled extremely far
The walls covered in complex stories
Of my past and present glories

A series of test I'll have to pass
Three or four almighty tasks
To guide me into the afterlife
Or descend deeper into darkness and strife

The walls have pictures of sphinxes
On the floor are jewels and riches
A grand pharaoh of my time
Scared and dismissed because of my crime.

Zoe Hyde (13)
Matravers School, Westbury

The Mummy

I'm lying here in my claustrophibic space,
Expression disappearing from my face,
Choking on the dust and standstorms,
Still waiting for Geb to weigh my heart
And let me bribe the gatekeepers to the Field of Reeds.

Still lying here in the blazing heat,
Feeling betrayed and broken,
Wondering if Osiris has forgotten me,
Now little more than a past memory
In a once great civilisation.

James McDonald (14)
Matravers School, Westbury

Summer

Heavenly colourful flowers open softly
Watch them sway and dance in the gentle wind . . .

Jostling queues scramble to line up,
Bustling for an exotic holiday.

Lick the drizzle of a temptingly tasty ice cream,
Rub the slippy, gooey suncream onto your burning skin.

Butterflies flit and flutter gracefully
Across beautifully pruned gardens,
Whilst bees buzz quietly up into the bright sky . . .

Let the radiant sun look down on you, smiling peacefully,
Bask in its warm, welcoming rays.

Watch caring mothers bathe in the sunlight,
Looking and smiling at their content children.

Summer is here . . .
And summer is wonderful!

Heather Evans (11)
St Laurence School, Bradford-on-Avon

I Know I Saw Her

I've never seen one before, not like her,
With her long, scarlet hair, bouncing behind her back,
Her watering, large eyes, mirroring the bright, blue sky,
I've never seen one before, never will again.

I think I saw her, fluttering behind the bed,
She was shimmering in the moonlight,
Her cheeky smile lighting up the room,
I've never seen one before, never will again.

I'm sure I saw her, lightly skipping across the lawn,
Gazing at the misty sky,
Dancing a musical dance,
I've never seen one before, never will again.

I know I saw her, twirling above my bed,
Little rosy-red lips,
Cheeks pale and untouched,
I've never seen one before, never will again.

I'm positive I saw her, playing in the pond,
Hiding behind the bulrushes,
Her reflection shining in the water,
I've never seen one before, never will again.

Of course I saw her, in a little pink tutu,
With sparkling earrings hanging from each ear,
Shiny shoes sitting on each foot,
I've never seen one before, never will again.

I wanted to see her, pattering across my floor,
Eyes sparkling, her smile lighting up the room,
She's gone, never to return,
Never seen one before, never will again.

Rosie Pearce (12)
St Laurence School, Bradford-on-Avon

The Man In The Moon

Living upon the stars,
Watching over the world,
Speaking in another voice,
Looking through another's eyes,
He's seen the ages of men,
He lives with nothing,
But silence to pass the time
And a feast of cheese,
Watching the seasons change
And the weather too,
But what a view!
A view of dreams,
Stars glistening, gleaming,
Planets hung like earrings of pearl,
Shooting stars are as familiar as smiles,
Where time slows,
A tick is a century
And a tock is a year,
A chime, oh a chime, last a lifetime,
But he wonders,
What there is down there?
And then one day,
He takes a step and lets go, leaves the moon behind,
He's flying through space, dropping down and down,
Stars passing by in a flash of silver,
But what's down there?
Well . . . I'll leave you to wonder and dream!

Eleanor Dodson (14)
St Laurence School, Bradford-on-Avon

Unicorn

When the crimson light floods the sky,
Into the sunset will fly
The most magnificent creature of all,
Tumbling melodies its call,
The shimmering sun, so bright,
She dances in the light,
Her silvery mane flows,
As pure as a budding white rose,
The scarlet sky turns gold,
As the long day grows old,
Her silver horn glows
And her true magic shows,
The dazzle inside rejoices!
Echoed by 1,000 voices,
The gold sky fades and dies,
The sorrow growing in her eyes,
The evening draws on,
The sun is now gone
And the sleeping unicorn
Awaits the dawn.

Esther Jewitt (12)
St Laurence School, Bradford-on-Avon

Depressed Boy

I see a kind person,
They ask me to play,
My sad, depressed mind
Says, 'Oh, go away!'

My mum cooks some tea,
So yum in your tum,
I shout out loud,
'It's disgusting, you scum!'

She buys me a present,
That any child should place proudly into their toy heap,
Oh no, not me,
'It's rubbish, it's cheap!'

I grow and I grow
And now I'm thirty
I'm still depressed
I'm sorry, I don't mean to be.

James Lewis (11)
St Laurence School, Bradford-on-Avon

Mum

Mum, the one who gives me love
Mum, like an angel from above
Mum, the one who gives me food
Mum, the one who calms me when in a mood
Mum, you can never be replaced
Mum, you're better than the human race
Mum, in all troubles you will pull me through
But you also must realise that I love you.

Jacob McKenzie (11)
The Crypt School, Gloucester

B-Unett

The girl I love, she always pushes me off,
Only because she thinks I'm a boff,
The truth is I really am not,
She just thinks I am.

She's too old for me,
That ain't gonna stop me, no,
Any way I can think,
I'll try to impress her.

I think she's bling, she thinks I'm ming,
I think she's hot, she thinks I'm not,
The way she shakes her hair and shows off her smile,
To get her, I'll run a mile.

She's too old for me,
That ain't gonna stop me, no,
Any way I can think of,
I'll try to impress her.

There's just one problem though,
She's two years older than me,
Maybe I should just give up on her,
I guess we were never meant to be.

She's too old for me,
That ain't gonna stop me, no
Anyway I can think of,
I'll try to impress her.

Henry Jordan (13)
The Crypt School, Gloucester

The Poppy Field

Somewhere in the countryside of France,
Lies a field covered in a blanket of poppies.
Like red dresses they dance through the summer breeze,
Their delicate petals like silk.
These flowers of beauty are a reminder of a curse,
So ugly that makes the brave veterans of our nation,
Our most treasured heroes.
Each blade of grass a soldier,
Determined to survive and the poppies are their fond memories,
The only comfort which they have left.
The wings of the radiant butterflies flap in the air,
Like regimental flags of war.
Gently they perch on the blood-red petals
And, unbeknown to their innocent selves, they pollinate them.
So now, every year, for many years,
Poppies will blanket this field,
Somewhere in the countryside of France.

Timothy Keasley (12)
The Crypt School, Gloucester

The Victim Of Bullies

I'm a victim of bullies
They punch me and tease me
They threaten to kill me
The leader also punches my mate, Steve.

They make my life a misery
I'm too scared to tell my mummy
I have marks all over
I just say I fell over in the shower.

My life has no direction
So I might as well end it now
I hope the bullies remember me
The pain and suffering they inflicted on me.

Elias McGill (12)
The Crypt School, Gloucester

War In The Air

The German air bomber, slowly flying above London
The sounds of guns shatter the still of the air
Thunderous noises terrorising little children
Bombs dropping, leaving devastation
Mass panic amongst the entire city
Even the guards are getting wary
Restless babies crying in their mother's arms
Shouting and screaming as loved ones fall to gunshots or bombs
Spitfires try to fend off wave upon wave of German aircraft
All you can hear is *crash! Bang! Boom!*
Gunfire is filling the scene
Along the street there is a stream of blood
Glass on the floor where the windowpanes have been shattered
Young boys and girls fleeing from London
All the parents are shouting is, 'Evacuation!'
German aircraft take down our planes
But we will keep on fighting until our dying day
We shall not surrender, we will not give in
And we will not be defeated
For we are British!

Michael Philpott (11)
The Crypt School, Gloucester

My Love

She came into my life two years ago,
We met by chance and I love her so.
She's cute and she's cuddly and brings such joy,
I'm lucky to be her special boy.
She looks at me with those puppy dog eyes,
When I leave her behind, you can hear her cries.
When I return home for tea,
She is so happy with glee.
I love her and cuddle her and give her a kiss,
She's someone I would never, ever snog,
As she's Willow, my faithful pet dog!

Liam Johnson (12)
The Crypt School, Gloucester

Seasons

Spring is when new life is made
And all bad memories begin to fade,
Many new things come to life
And wave goodbye to all last year's strife.

Summer is hot, sticky and fun,
It's when the holiday's just begun,
You go away, close or abroad
And it's very unlikely that you'll get bored.

Autumn is cold and dead leaves fall
And no one is very well at all,
It's Hallowe'en season, very spooky and scary,
But on the wet pavement, you must be wary.

Winter is amazing, exciting but cold
And when many, many items are rapidly sold
And Santa comes down our tall chimney
And he places some presents down, under the tree.

The outcome of seasons cannot be told,
But you will soon find out, as the weather unfolds.

Ieuan Prosser (11)
The Crypt School, Gloucester

My Most Prized Possession - My Bed

Tired is how you make me feel,
Here I eat my every meal.
'Lie on me!' is what you say,
I sleep on you every day.
Lying on you makes me calm,
But what I hate most, is that stupid
Alarm!

Callum Holder (11)
The Crypt School, Gloucester

Abandoned

All alone, cold, wet and hungry
Why did they leave me here
All on my own?
Death's arms were about to close on me
But like a wounded soldier, I fought on
Through the rain and rubble
Wind and waste
Nobody wanted me and if I died
Nobody would remember me.
Specks of hope enlightened my mind
Will I be saved or will I die?
All was lost, but I was to be found
As morning crept over the horizon
Workers came flooding in
The quarry was busy and as our eyes crossed
I barked and bounded towards him
I had found my new home.

James Keasley (12)
The Crypt School, Gloucester

The Christmas Light

I woke up today, it was Christmas morning,
I woke up today and looked out on the day dawning,
I woke up today, stretching and yawning,
I woke up today, on Christmas morning!

I ran down the stairs, as fast as I could,
I ran down the stairs, throwing off my gown hood,
I ran down the stairs, knowing the day would be good,
I ran down the stairs, as fast as I could!

I shouted out loud, 'Merry Christmas to all!'
I shouted out loud, 'Do not fight, do not duel!'
I shouted out loud, ''Tis the season of Yule!'
I shouted out loud, 'Merry Christmas to all!'

I woke up today, on Christmas morning,
I woke up today and looked out on the day dawning,
I woke up today, stretching and yawning,
I woke up today, it was Christmas morning!

Tom Thornes (12)
The Crypt School, Gloucester

Chelsea, Chelsea FC

Chelsea, Chelsea,
We are on fire,
The rest are dire,
We're the best, that's true,
The colour to wear is blue,
We are well psyched,
But we are hated, not liked,
We want respect,
You're OK, we're select,
Oh, what a volley by Frankie,
I bet you're upset, get out your hankie,
There's a substitution Cole,
On for a minute, oh what a goal!
1-0 down, 5-1 up
And we're going to win every single cup!

Jack Brickell (12)
The Crypt School, Gloucester

Daily Life

The school bell rings
The day begins
The lessons start
We're all very smart

German to maths
RE and art
The subjects are good
We all do as we should

Crypt is great
There's no debate
We have fun
Rain or sun

When the last lesson ends
We say goodbye to our friends
We catch the bus home
Talking on the phone.

Jack Woodward (11)
The Crypt School, Gloucester

The Breach

The evil spy of Saruman awaits,
To hear the wishes of the white wizard.
He knows that he cannot defeat the king,
When he defends the mighty keep, Helm's Deep.
He wishes that the mighty king would flee,
For the wizard Saruman is plotting,
Plotting to destroy the kingdom of Man.
He sends his army of ten thousand strong,
Knowing that the king can't defend his keep.
For Saruman has found out the weakness,
The weakness that will end the world of man.

The outer wall is made of solid rock,
But for one part which is no more than wood.

The king knows that his men will not see dawn,
Because the ranger, Aragorn, foretold.
He sends the men and boys to armour up
And puts them in the defence of the keep.

The women and babes are sent to the caves,
Where they realise that they cannot be harmed.

A horn is heard, but not an Orc horn, no!
It is the horn of the Elvish people,
Who have come to honour an allegiance,
An allegiance that once stood between them.
Patience looms in the atmosphere, they're scared!

Simon Laird (15)
The Crypt School, Gloucester

The Shadow Of Life

I hear you call my name
Your whispers in the air
The shadow of your image came
And warmed me with your prayer
I watched you grow to the world
But no one showed you pride
I watched you beauty as it unfurled
And I remained at your side
I loved you for what you were
And hoped you felt the same
But then your voice had changed
And no longer spoke my name
You mourned the love of another soul
Another better than I
No matter how I felt
I knew I shouldn't cry
You were the one I cared for
When the world thought you a toy
After the world had torn at you
You had finally found joy
And as he came and took you away
I felt so empty inside
I was alone on this wasteland
With only the shadow of the rose
And the emptiness by my side.

Trystan Archer (15)
The Crypt School, Gloucester

My Only Teddy

My teddy has something to share
Love, compassion, nothing compares
It's soft wool by my side
Tender, warm and hope inside
Helps me on my ride to nowhere
But I know I'm going somewhere.

My teddy has a meaning to me
My hope glows up as big as a tree
It makes me wonder about the meaning of life
Cutting through the earth with a knife
Throwing it in the wind of air
It is the one, I will always care.

My teddy has a life of its own
Whether it's funny, happy or all alone
It makes me think and look in the sky
Every time I talk, it only says, 'Why?'
My lifeless but happy trustworthy friend
This is the poem that will never end.

Nicholas Walker (11)
The Crypt School, Gloucester

Good And Bad People

I am a burglar, stealing in the night,
I am a burglar, what I do is *not* right.

I am a fireman, saving in the night,
I am a fireman, what I do *is* right.

I am a shoplifter, nicking things in the day
I am a shoplifter, I take but I *don't* pay.

I am a policeman, nicking people in the day,
I am a policeman, people caught *will* pay.

I am a pickpocket, what you've got I take,
I am a pickpocket, *dishonest* money I make.

I am a security warden, I see what you take,
I am a security warden, *honest* money I make.

Some people are bad,
When they should be good.
To all in the world I say you should:
Do what's right and not what's wrong,
Then we all can get along.

Edward Kingston (11)
The Crypt School, Gloucester

Really Ill

A tissue, a tissue,
I really need the loo,
I am so ill, I chucked up over Phil,
Yes I am really ill, I am really ill.

A tissue, a tissue,
Splitter, splatter, splot!
I really need a tissue,
Splatter, splitter, snot!

I really need the loo,
A plop a doodle doo,
There is a rumble, grumble in my belly
It feels all tingly, like jelly.

I was so ill, I chucked up over Phil
So he's extremely ill,
Today I am on the mend
I hope he's still my friend!

Yes, he's really ill, he's really ill!

Ben Williams (11)
The Crypt School, Gloucester

Sightseeing

When I walked across the pier,
I listened to what I could see and hear,
People walked by, chatting away,
Then I thought to myself, *what a nice day!*

I started to walk over the sand,
Then a couple went by hand in hand,
Then I sat down on a bench,
Suddenly it started to rain and . . .
I got drenched!

As I walked home,
People stopped and stared
And whispered to each other
That's Adam Beard.

When I got in I turned on the TV,
To see what was on before I cooked tea,
Then I jumped into bed,
I fell asleep and it looked like I was dead.

Russell Beacham (12)
The Crypt School, Gloucester

Lost Hope

Today was the day, after hours of silent battles in my head
About whether or not I should ask her
I felt sick in my stomach, like an iron weight was in my stomach
And was gaining weight every second
I loved everything about her
From her sparkling sapphire eyes, to her chestnut hair
Which gave the smell of a newly blossomed rose
Every day my mind would wander into a helpless dream
And only being brought back to Earth
When my teacher clapped her hands
When I am near her, my mind goes into deep space
And I lose the power of speech
Before doing something stupid and embarrassing
But today was the day
No more putting it off
I had hit my barrier and now was my time to climb it
I stood up in my seat, sliding backwards
I walked over to her table
Each step causing my heart to slam against my ribs
Like it was trying to break out
Even though she was only three metres away
And the chatter was loud
It felt like a was running a marathon, wearing earmuffs
I could smell her sweet smell, as I drew ever closer to her table
Then out of nowhere, somebody came over
And asked if she would go out with him
I waited a few moments to let those three letters hit home
Yes! I couldn't believe it
How could I have been so stupid
To think she would go somewhere with me?
It felt like an iron hand had gripped my heart
A cold, iron hand clenching my heart
I returned to my seat, drained of everything
I had lost all hope.

Rupert Milward-Wiffen (12)
The Crypt School, Gloucester

Friendship

A friend is someone you can trust,
A friend is someone you get to know, everyone needs to be happy,
There are some people who don't have friends to be happy,
There are some people who don't have any friends,
They can be boys and girls.
You have to treat friends with respect,
You might get to meet a girl if she is your friend
And decide to go out with them.

A friend is not someone who is an enemy,
You can turn this around if you take time to get to know them.
You mustn't treat friends badly,
You don't know when you might need them to help you.

I have lots of friends
They make me happy when I am sad,
Friendship matters to me!

Scott Gardner (14)
The Priory School, Taunton

MC Price

My name is MC Price
I spit two lyrics as I come by your house
Remember there's a price to pay for the pain
You put me through
So don't say it's for the best because everyone
Can change once in a while.
So don't try to play me
Because you social workers can't change us
Only we can do that so let us go home
Please, we did not come for the pain we came
Into the world to be loved not numbered.

Joel Price (15)
The Priory School, Taunton

The Priory

One day I woke up for school
Intent on breaking every rule

I woke up at twenty to eight
My mum shouted that I was going to be late

No time for breakfast, just a fag!
My mum had a go at me, nag, nag, nag

Into the taxi not far to go
Even though he's driving slow

Arrive at school feeling good
Sweeney says, 'Take down that hood!'

That does it, now he'll pay
I'm going to spoil his brilliant day

I go into first lesson, feeling bad
Miss Addison said, 'Get out your folder!'
I think she's mad

I survived till break and got my tuck
The book's gone missing, there's been a ruck

Maths is next, I don't want to go
I'm no good with numbers, the lesson goes slow

Lunch is next, I'm going off site
I said to my mate, 'Have you got a light?'

Now I'm back, ready to work
But I don't like the teacher, he's a jerk

Now it's options, playing football
Now football's over, end of school.

Colin Walls (15)
The Priory School, Taunton

Inside

Life and death
Who decides?
Dark and light
Show me the way
Ying and yang
Inner peace
At one with the world.

Michael Harmer (15)
The Priory School, Taunton

A Recipe For Me

First of all, I'd take some friends
And put them in the pan and then I'd stir some fun
Into a big fat cherry bun
I'd mix some clothes and high-heeled shoes into a custard pie
I'd leave to simmer in the air while serving up my fry
I'd mix myself a cash delight
While watching my cat eat Marmite
I'd scoff and lounge all day long
While baking a cake with laughs and songs
I'd slurp up strawberry milkshake with a hint of animals
While baking in a saucepan all the shopping malls.

Georgia Watts (11)
Thomas Keble School, Stroud

A Recipe For Me!

Take my model trains play with them around the house
Add my model magazines as I read them around the fire
Leave to play with my Lego models
Mix my bike in as well so I can cycle all day long
I will cook in the baking heat of the sun
While it's best to serve with lots and lots of presents.

Peter Moore (11)
Thomas Keble School, Stroud

A Recipe For Chelsea

Ingredients
Fun
Smiles
Humour
Attitude
Naughtiness
Friends
Oven
Laughs

Take some fun and add lots of smiles,
Mix a sense of humour,
Beat in some attitude,
Oven bake with some friends,
Leave to rise and apply some icing of laughs,
Bake until nice and happy,
Sprinkle on a bit of naughtiness,
Serve with a piece of cake and relax.

Chelsea Hall (11)
Thomas Keble School, Stroud

A Recipe For Me!

Ingredients
A family
A holiday
Sun
Love
Car

Take a well loved family and a very hot day
Add a well-earned meal
Mix with other families
Boil with excitement
Leave to enjoy
Serve with a lot of love.

Emma Jones (11)
Thomas Keble School, Stroud

A Recipe For Me

Ingredients
Two metres of flesh
180 bones
Some organs
Two eyes
One nose
Five litres of water
And a barrel of fun and friendship

Take the bones and set them out
But please try getting it right
Then add the organs
Add the flesh but please try and do it properly
Mix in the water until 70% of me is full
Mature for 11-12 years
Leave to cool before use
Serve with a barrel of fun and friendship.

Rebecca Fagg (11)
Thomas Keble School, Stroud

A Recipe For Me

Take one Fraser
Add a library
And an endless amount of food and drink
Then read lots and lots and lots of books
Throw in a play with my mates, but mostly reading

Sprinkle with a ticket to Lazerland
Boil up a day of school
Mix until satisfied with day.

Serve with . . . a trip to the cinema.

Fraser McLeod (11)
Thomas Keble School, Stroud

A Recipe For Me

Take a bucket full of books,
Shove in a couple of cats and dogs,
Mix them with a lot of artwork
And also a lot of taps for dancing!
Bake in your favourite treats and sweets
Leave to cool in a swimming pool,
Add some chocolate friendship icing,
Then finally, sprinkle on some sugar
And also a dose of mints!

Hannah Rickards (11)
Thomas Keble School, Stroud

A Recipe For Me

Take a few chips, add some coffee
Then stick a computer and an Xbox in the bowl.
Get a selection of cats and my family
Then sieve a load of ghost stories and mix them all together.
Then shove it in the microwave for five minutes
And leave it for one minute
And serve it with a load of kindness.

Liam Lines (11)
Thomas Keble School, Stroud

The Fish

Bubble blower
Swift swimmer
Wave knower
Golden glimmer
Food fetcher
Feature fester
Fin flapper.

Nathan Piper (12)
Thomas Keble School, Stroud

Pike

Pike
Fish snatcher
Advantage taker
Lure cruncher
Fish napper
Scale scratcher
Death bringer
Invisible sniper
Quick striker
Flesh puncturer
Sly ambusher
Line breaker
Bone cruncher
Roach snapper
Blood sucker
Family murderer
Prey devourer
Serial killer.

Hayden Scamp (13)
Thomas Keble School, Stroud

Cheetah

Big gunner
Fast runner
Tear dropper
Jungle copper
Spotty fur
Loud purr
Wet nose
Strike a pose
Large paws
Big jaws
Huge eyes
No lies!

Ellen Trueman (12)
Thomas Keble School, Stroud

Then You Were There

I feel your hand touch mine,
A shiver runs up my spine,
I turn around,
You're not there.

Dreams, dreams, dreams,
Everything happens in dreams,
I thought you were there,
But you weren't.

Oh my God!
It's real life now,
I can see you behind me,
You're getting closer.

I feel you hand touch mine,
A shiver runs up my spine,
I turn around,
You're there!

Maizey Roberts (14)
Thomas Keble School, Stroud

Rattlesnake

Victim seeker
Prison keeper
Silent striker
Sun liker
Rule breaker
Death maker
Salsa shaker
Life taker!
Rattlesnake!

Gracie Fickling (12)
Thomas Keble School, Stroud

The Door
(Based on 'The Door' by Miroslav Holub)

Go and open the door
Maybe inside there's
A 3D world with everything perfect and nothing going wrong
Go and open the door
There could be a world where aliens rule
Where no one is free
Where no plants grow
Where people's minds are sucked right out of them
Go and open the door
There could be a world where there is nothing, just black
Where there is no night and no day
No sun and no moon
No Earth and no sky
Go and open the door
There could just be your bedroom.

Tim Coysh (12)
Thomas Keble School, Stroud

A Snake

Floor slitherer
Menace maker
Mice eater
Egg stealer
Invisible serpent
Heat seeker
Poison biter
Nest invader
Forked tongued
Beady eyed
Scaly skinned.

James Mahdiyone (12)
Thomas Keble School, Stroud

A House In Westward Road

Big and tall,
In Ebley,
A conservatory,
Toys in it,
A PlayStation 2 like a games console,
House smells fresh as a daisy,
Dog called Paddy,
Rabbits called Nibbles and Smurf,
Full of dog hairs,
Kitchen smells of dogs,
Dog is lively as a clown,
It barks when excited,
My house is like a bouncy castle,
Two gerbils called Blacky and Fudge,
Got a pond like a lake.

Sam Coxhead (11)
Thomas Keble School, Stroud

Hamsters

Wheel runners
Apple lovers
Cute stunners
Shredding covers
Chipping floor
Metal door
Day sleepers
Night wakers
One brown
Two grey
My hamsters.

Kristina Peart (12)
Thomas Keble School, Stroud

Bonfire Night

Bonfire Night is fun, fun, fun,
The noises are like shots from a gun.
Shining, swirling, sparkling lights,
Brightening up those dull, dull nights.

The whining, screaming noises they make,
Keep all the boring neighbours awake.
As they're fired into the air,
Everyone waits and stands to stare.

Glittering, gleaming, shining bright,
The fireworks bang next to the moonlight.
Dashing quickly up from the ground,
Whirling, swirling, round and round.

The children get scared from what they hear
As the bang and the sparks is what they fear.
Fireworks are great when treated with care,
But they're extremely dangerous, so you had better beware.

The people sadly go home to bed,
The thoughts of the fireworks still rushing through their head.
The night has ended with a big bang and a cheer
And that is it, until next year!

Helena Short (14)
Thomas Keble School, Stroud

Hawk

Good glider
Tidy hider
Life taker
Time maker
Wind hoverer
Song lover
Born leader
Youth feeder.

Liam Horsley (12)
Thomas Keble School, Stroud

Tabbit

If you walk in the jungle
You might hear something
A little, tiny rabbit
Will jump to your feet
It's a tiny body, with long, long legs
It hops, it jumps, it goes everywhere about
It's the Tabbit, the Tabbit, the Tabbit!

It's small and grey
With large teeth
And if you're mean to the tiny Tabbit
It might just eat your feet
It's the Tabbit, the Tabbit, the Tabbit!

The Tabbit jumps so high
To catch its prey
It nibbles at carrots, grass,
Lettuce and hay
They run and run around in pairs
Hopping and jumping all over the place
Their tails flash, flash, flash away
As they hop across the fields today.

Georgia Wood (12)
Thomas Keble School, Stroud

The Golden Beast

Animal killer
Meat ripper
Yellow stalker
Blood gorger
Sudden pouncer
Deep growler
Animal slayer
Talented destroyer
Animal tracker
Well-known slaughterer
The lion is the king of the jungle.

Lucy Wise (12)
Thomas Keble School, Stroud

Prejudice

Striving for the world to be a better place for everyone,
But will we ever see this world?

A better place is where there is no crime,
No cheating,
No racism,
No drugs,
No alcohol,
No prejudice,
Just a beautiful place for all.

A prejudiced place is where there is prejudices against blacks,
Whites,
Teenagers,
Disabled children,
Elderly people,
Just a horrible place for all.

Will we ever see such a better place?
My guess
No!

A better place is a dream . . .
A prejudiced place is reality!

Charlotte Granger (14)
Thomas Keble School, Stroud

Dog Kennings

Cat chaser
Dog racer
Food lover
Warm cover
Barking mad
Eyes sad
Walk taker
Mess maker
Loyal friend
Until the end!

Abi Wilkins & Fleur Tanner (12)
Thomas Keble School, Stroud

The Snow Fields
(For Floppy 1994-2001)

In the freezing cold landscape
Where nothing grows
Lie the snow fields
Lying still - with no signs of life.
In the blank, mysterious landscape
Where it's dire and hard to see
Lie the snow fields
Lying still - unable to move.
In the frosty, harsh landscape
Where it's deep and hard to move
Lie the snow fields
Lying still - in pain on this dying world.
In the flat and thick landscape
Where it's almost impossible to live
Lie the snow fields
Lying still - all soft and fluffy.
In the ferocious, frosty landscape
Where all life seems to be gone
Lie the snow fields
Lying still - just waiting to die.
In the warm heat of my old bedroom
I kept him with me - close to me
By my side, hoping he could hold on
But he didn't, he couldn't.
Now all I have are memories
He's gone, no longer with me
Like the snow fields, he's no one's
He was mine.
He was happy when he was mine
And I hope he's happy now as well
You cured my blindness, I can see clearly now
I thank you; Floppy.

Tyrone Keene (14)
Thomas Keble School, Stroud

Dog Fish

Flip, flap, woof, woof, dog fish is here,
He wags his fin and licks your face,
He always undoes your shoelace
He can go underwater
And see you later.

When he's underwater
He blows bubbles.
He can hear when you call him
He's always happy to see you.

Flip, flap, woof, woof, dog fish is here,
When he leaves he gives you a tear.
Rub his tummy and give him some honey.
Such a happy dog fish,
Everyone could have one if they wish.

Jess Cox (12)
Thomas Keble School, Stroud

A Recipe For Me

Take a light dappled forest
Snow-covered mountains and ancient warriors
Mix with a large cliff
Pour on a skateboard ramp
Add cracked skulls and old leather
Sprinkle with Green Day clips
Stir in some sea-blue and forest-green
Boil with Elvish ears
Sieve in surf-tipped waves, then leave to soak
Leave to cool, then serve with good friends.

Finn Thomas-Cooney (11)
Thomas Keble School, Stroud

A Recipe For Me

I'd add a pinch of sunshine
I'd have a pint of red wine
I'd stir in some friends
I'd cook it till it ends.
I'd get a load of dough
I'd make my own film called, 'Go Go.'
I'd boil it till 12 o'clock
I'd have a party with a piñata sock
Now this is over
But don't forget . . . me!

Amii Hughes (11)
Thomas Keble School, Stroud

A Recipe For Fay

I have dark brown hair and brown eyes
I can be cheeky too
Mix is some music, my favourite is Eminem
Add some pets, two cats, two gerbils, one puppy and ten fish
My family - one sister, four brothers, Mum and Stepdad
I have a bedroom it is small
But cool with pink and purple hearts.

Fay Hughes (12)
Thomas Keble School, Stroud

A Recipe For Me

Take a bundle of blonde hair
A pair of blue eyes
Add a cheeky grin
And mix with some friends
Mix with some Akon
And the noise is locked up
Mix with chips and curry.

Charlotte Lane (11)
Thomas Keble School, Stroud

A Recipe For Me

Take a boy with a naughty streak and a sense of humour,
Take 1,000,000,000 tons of sugar to compare with him,
Take drum and bass and rap,
Kind, polite, never fights, always hyper, not a football fan,
Rugby is the game that is all you need.

Place the boy on the playground,
Sprinkle the sugar over the playground like snow,
Shove the drum and bass and rap in the boy's head,
Mix all the others together.

What will you get?

Liam Summers (11)
Thomas Keble School, Stroud

How To Make An Eleanor Cairns

Take a pinch of fun
Mix to a creamy mixture of joy and hope
Add some blonde hair and blue eyes
Bake until good and happy
Leave to rise until it's really healthy
Serve with some good mates.

Eleanor Cairns (11)
Thomas Keble School, Stroud

A Recipe For Me

Take one song from Limp Bizkit
Add a few grams of Predator and stir in one Alien.
Fold in a pistol and an M16 rifle
And put a drizzle of blood and gore
And finally a drop of PS2 games.

Tom Carpenter (12)
Thomas Keble School, Stroud

The Liadiator

It will roar when you turn it on and off
It will frighten you then keep you warm
It will walk around king of the pride
It will stay warm and keep your house warm
It will keep your house heated in summer
It will obey your every command
It will change the heat if you ask it to
It will act like a pet but never touch
Or you may be in for a bit of a fright.

Ashley Garraway (12)
Thomas Keble School, Stroud

Friends

Friends, they're all around
When you're down
They give you a hug
They try not to bug.
They're always there, they do always care
They hope for the best
Don't give it a rest
Until you're high up in the air.

Charlotte Watkins (14)
Thomas Keble School, Stroud

Bracelands

My bedroom is as purple as lavender
My hallway is as white as snow
My brother's room is as blue as a whale
My outhouse is as brown as chocolate
Our house is as big as my old primary school
Our garden is full of toys
Our front garden is as small as a car.

Stacey Cantillion (11)
Thomas Keble School, Stroud

Life On The Stage

The stress of rehearsals
Spending day after day
Going over my lines
So I know what to say.

One week till the big day
All the hard work we put in
Is now coming to an end
The real stress now begins.

The night of the show
And the crowd is growing fast
Backstage people are preparing
Their moment has come at last.

I step out onto the stage
The crowd is silent, the lights are bright
I take a deep breath and shout,
'Hello, how is everyone tonight?'

When I'm on the stage
I feel I'm at home
When the curtains go down
I'm left on my own.

The sound of the crowd
Like they're roaring with rage
There's no feeling quite like it
Like life on the stage.

Rhianne Banyard (14)
Thomas Keble School, Stroud

Cinquains

Kittens,
Very playful
And also very cute,
They like to muck around and bounce,
Kittens.

Puppies,
Soft and fluffy,
Playful during the day,
Sleepy and helpless at night-time,
Puppies.

Cheetahs,
Big and spotty
And like to bounce around,
They like to catch their prey, they're proud,
Cheetahs.

Tigers,
Are really cute
And also really big,
They really like to eat raw meat
And play.

Donkeys,
Slow and sleepy,
They like to eat their hay,
You always see them on the beach,
Donkeys.

Amy Clark & Safaya Sutton (13)
Thomas Keble School, Stroud

Cinquains

Panda
Is black and white
They live out in the wild
They eat leaves from their habitat
Bamboo

Puppies
Are very cute
They are very lively
Puppies have pointed little teeth
Ouch, ouch!

Rabbits
They are fluffy
Also they are jumpy
They are lazy and very shy
Rabbits

Monkey
They are cheeky
They like to climb high trees
Monkeys like to eat lots of leaves
Yummy!

Kittens
Very playful
And also very cute
They like to mooch around and bounce
Kittens.

Laura Wilkes (13)
Thomas Keble School, Stroud

The Leopard

The slender creature slinking through the tall-deprived grass
Staring at the silenced beauty of the hunted
The target is in clear view
However, the hunter goes unnoticed
Slowly, slyly, stalking its prey through the bush
Its natural camouflage helping it to remain a figment of imagination
You don't know it's there until it's too late . . .

Wham! . . . You're stuck to the ground
Your airway pierced
Struggling for air
Suffocating
Your heart pounding in your ears
The heavy burden of its paws on your chest,
So heavy, but I know it's going to be quick
These few seconds feel like an age to me,
I see myself,
My life and then my future
Lying in a tree, only a snack for later
I'll last.
His prey.

I am the hunter of the grass,
The hunted!

Laura Bellamy (14)
Thomas Keble School, Stroud

The Cob'e'ment

It sits
In the corner
Staring at its prey
You try to dust it, it scares you away
It glares at you every single day
If you try to move it, it will say
'Don't remove me, the cob'e'ment,' I should stay
If you try you will certainly pay.

John-Paul Crawford (12)
Thomas Keble School, Stroud

The Dolfish Tank

This isn't an ordinary fish tank;
'Cause you may find it in a bank.

It is in the shape of a dolphin,
But without all of its fins!

Inside the big blue dolphin,
There are fish the size of the pin!

The dolphin is a light shade of blue,
But there are only a few!

Johanna Barton (12)
Thomas Keble School, Stroud

Cadio

Watch out for the cadio,
It screeches really loud.
If you hear it
Run as fast as you can.
For if you hear the cadio
You will get put in a trance.

You will dance all over the place
Know every word to every song
You will never be normal again . . .

Sophie Dewhurst (12)
Thomas Keble School, Stroud

Cinquain

The horse
It is running
Free in the wild forest
On his back is a saddle and
Rider.

Joshua Todd (13)
Thomas Keble School, Stroud

Giant Quanda

It goes further fast
And it is the last.
It eats bamboo
And might get you.

It comes in a crate
It does not have a mate.
It's going to be extinct
So do not blink.

So you think you are riding a quad
And you like giant pandas
You might just be riding a . . .
Quanda!

Matthew Austin (12)
Thomas Keble School, Stroud

Monitor Cube

Beware! Beware! He lurks in the deep!
The monitor cube will eat your feet
He waits and waits till his prey comes along
Happy and fierce and feeling strong
He gobbles them up
And spits out their feet!

Jordan Sowerby (13)
Thomas Keble School, Stroud

The Dragonfleaf

The Dragonfleaf swoops in and out the trees,
All the time it carries insects on its leaves.
Every season it changes colour,
But in winter the colour gets duller.

Alana Curtis (12)
Thomas Keble School, Stroud

Cinquains

The beach
Hot and sunny
Swishy waves, fun and gold
People gathering and playing
The beach

Seasons
Winter snowflakes
The flowers blooming out
The golden leaves swaying in wind
Hot days.

Nicole Mallett (13)
Thomas Keble School, Stroud

Monplayer

Watch out for the monplayer
Because when you put the headphones in your ears
It tickles you and screams
It won't let you turn off
Or turn the next music channel on
Only let's you listen to
Monkeys in the jungle
So watch out for this cheeky monkey
Or else you will never be normal again!

Bille Marie Dimino (12)
Thomas Keble School, Stroud

My Nan

My nan was like a big bear always ready for a hug
I can still taste her delicious trifles
She was great at puzzles
It was always a race to fit the last bit
She always had time for me
But like a clock, she stopped.

Alice Gregory (11)
Thomas Keble School, Stroud

Clonkey

The forest is the strangest place
With many creatures with strange hands and face.
Amongst many of these misfits
Are monkeys made of many bits.
Some with cogs and some with teeth
And some with talons like a beast.

But there is one in general called a clonkey
Partly a clock and partly a monkey.
You mustn't fear this crazy design
Because it's gentle, so it's fine.

With a pendulum for a tail and hands on its face
It swings through the trees with style and grace.
Ticking and tocking wherever it goes
Why and how they were made, nobody knows.

As night falls it climbs up a tree
Ticking and tocking itself to sleep.
Clicking and clanking into the morn
Waking with a tick and a yawn.

As he wakes in the morn with a bit of a surprise
To see something in front of him with large green eyes.
He loses his grip and slips out of the tree
And falls to his death on the cold floor beneath.

Luckily his pendulum got caught in a branch
Saved him from death, giving him a second chance.
Now the clonkey lives in an oak tree
With some birds and his family.

Amy Goldstone (12)
Thomas Keble School, Stroud

Dable

As you sit at the desk today,
Something will always be watching you,
But don't panic, don't be scared,
Just beware today at school.
Suddenly in the lesson before lunch
You hear a tummy-like rumble,
But don't be too sure, it's probably the *dable!*

You will find that you are not sitting at an ordinary table,
You are sitting at a magic dable.
It will do some work for you
But it will always want a thank you.
Dable is very powerful; it will never give up
It will always have the answers
The dable looks like any other table
You cannot see his head and tail
Except when there is nobody or just you.

Don't forget when the year ends
Dable might still be wandering around.
It might even come back to you again
Or someone else might have the joy of him.
But just beware, dable will always
Be *there!*

Megan Laws (12)
Thomas Keble School, Stroud

Croco Beans

If it's something you've not seen,
Let me tell you about the croco bean,
It's like a bean in a baked bean tin,
But the bean has got a crocodile in

If you want to grow some crocs,
Get yourself some beans in a box,
Croco bean, water, grow,
Watch these beans aren't slow.

Angus McCrindle (12)
Thomas Keble School, Stroud

Cinquains

The beach
Sandy, golden
Swishy waves hot, foamy
People gathering and playing
Castles

Seasons
Winter snowflakes
The flowers blooming out
The golden leaves swaying in wind
Hot days

Nature
Little bunnies
Wild animals running
Big, grassy fields and wild mushrooms
Long days.

Catherine Marsden (14)
Thomas Keble School, Stroud

The Horde

You will ride the Horde
*But you won't ride
The Horde again!*

Because your death has
Dawned.

You may think it's safe
But don't be fooled
Because inside a blade sleeps.

When you sit on the Horde
The blade awakens and all that will be left
Is a puddle of blood and a *body!*

Adam Pinkney (12)
Thomas Keble School, Stroud

My Cat - Cinquains

My cat
Is very quick
Runs and runs into the kitchen
Yum-yum

Eats mice
Catches some more
Mice; goes back inside and
Eats it up and goes to sleep. Cat
Is tired!

Wakes up
Then goes upstairs
He knows that he isn't
Allowed up there, Get cross with him.
Shoo cat!

He sneaks
Again and tries
To go upstairs and he
Goes to my bedroom. Sleeps all day
Snoring

Cat fight
In the garden
Jumps and pounces on each
Other. They miaow when they fight.
Stay back!

Ben Hassan (14)
Thomas Keble School, Stroud

Portable Moo Player

If you are ever on your own
In the mountains of moo,
You should always look out
For the portable moo player.

It swings from tree to tree,
Nothing is as it seems, as it is free,
It comes out behind you
And starts to play music.

Then . . . he jumps on top of you
And starts to lick your face,
As he puts you in his face,
He starts to trot along.

And when you are eaten
He starts to play a song!

Kenny Walker (12)
Thomas Keble School, Stroud

It's The Chiv

Here is the Chiv
The only Chiv in the barn
If you walk into one
You see something very suspicious
It's the Chiv.
It has blazing beak, big feet, a fuzzy belly
And wings that could knock you out.

The Chiv moves as fast as lightning
It's as rich as Bill Gates
It's as fat as Henry the VIII
And it could eat you in one gulp.

Joe Dickenson (13)
Thomas Keble School, Stroud

Shores Of Pain

It moved closer swirling towards land,
Turning, twisting and shaving the sand,
Like a giant claw it took all in its way,
As on the seabed like a monster it lay,
Hideous and terrifying it rose up and swept,
Everything in sight, spilling rain as it wept,
Innocent people scattered here and there,
But in the end none were to spare,
It rose up and destroyed everything bright,
The people, the trees, the stars and the light,
As it massed in the sky, one giant black cloud,
No prisoners did this storm allow,
Then it went as soon as it came,
Destruction it left on the shores of pain.

Gabriel Raeburn (14)
Thomas Keble School, Stroud

Telephant

If you go into your lounge
Where your telephant is
Turn it on but don't press the wrong button
Or you will be soaked!

The two ears are the speakers
They are big
So be careful how loud you want your telephant!

The remote control is in the shape
Of an elephant's trunk.

Rebecca Wallington (12)
Thomas Keble School, Stroud

What To Call A Cat

Speedy jumper
Tree lover
Flea bag
Fun player
Fast runner
Bright eyes
Loud purer
Mouse hunter
Claw extender
Heavy sleeper
Bird trapper
Big pounces
Dinner lover
Human lover
Spring jumper
Food scrounger
Sneaky hunter
Fluff ball
Sneaky devil
Human beggar
People scrounger.

Sam Nash (12)
Thomas Keble School, Stroud

Turike

Scaly bike the turtle Turike
Don't confuse it for a bike.

Be safe when you brake
Or you might fall into a lake.

A turtle and a bike
Are made to form a Turike.

So remember when you ride a bike
This poem about a Turike.

Sam Evans (12)
Thomas Keble School, Stroud

The Battle

The sky was frightening
People were dying and screaming.
The ground was shaking
The food was horrible, it tasted like mud.
The smell was horrific, it made me sick
They touched the ground like scared little children.
I could taste the air as I walked past
The sounds were deafening
They made my ears dent.
I had my horrible food again
It made my stomach turn.
My eyes were watering
My body was soaking.
It made my hands yucky
My head was spinning.
I made my arms fall to the ground
My face was horrible
It made me feel smelly.
My nose was funny
It made my nose feel like a plate of jelly.

Gemma Dianne Scrivens (14)
Thomas Keble School, Stroud

Tigertar

If you walk in the jungle,
Don't go far,
Because somewhere deep in,
There is a Tigertar.

When you hear some music,
Make sure you run,
Because if he hears you,
He's going to have a lot of fun!

Jordan Frapwell (12)
Thomas Keble School, Stroud

In The Eye Of Katrina

The wind howls the bitter song of death, forever lashing
The flood drowns and rips, all consuming
And the savage lightning strikes, killing and burning
Overhead the thunder shouts hellishly rumbling
Through the night air echoes the sound of people screaming
Onward, onward the water's always advancing
Forward, forward the beast menacingly roaring
Now comes the peace of the light dawning
But is split by the shriek of a child crying
As she watches her mother drift by, dead and floating
People stare is disbelief, aimlessly watching
Abandoned and alone, the hunger creeping
Man and child alike sat in the homes waiting and weeping
For a rescue that doesn't seem to be coming.

Tadhg Martin-Haydock (14)
Thomas Keble School, Stroud

The Door
(Inspired by 'The Door' by Miroslav Holub)

Go open the door, maybe there is a magnificent chocolate factory
The best in the world
No lorries polluting the air
Just men on bikes at the dead of night
Smoke coming from the chimneys
But it's the sweet smell of mouth-watering chocolate
It's almost hypnotising the villages with such a sweet smell
Of butterscotch and hot fudge fingers
Can you smell the chocolate
Coming from the crack in the door?

Timothy Williams (12)
Thomas Keble School, Stroud

The Dolbed

The dolbed is warm and bright
Just like a light.
It is bright and blue
Just like the sea.

When you jump upon the dolbed
Will it flip you with its flipper?
It is great and kind
Just like the calm, warm ocean.

When you jump on the dolbed
It is bouncy like a bouncy castle.
It's fun to play with
Just like a friend.

Lisa Brown (12)
Thomas Keble School, Stroud

The Brambles

Called The Brambles
Smells like wet dog
Rooms are small as a pond
Has not got a chimney
Has a dog called Molly
And a cat called Moppet
One cat called Mittens, died
My room's as small as a box
Dog needs lots of walks
Brothers - got two
Got a PlayStation 2
The garden is as tiny as a cabbage
Got a shed, long and thin, like banana.

Oliver Jefferies (11)
Thomas Keble School, Stroud

Eagleotch

Tick . . . flap . . . tick . . . flap . . . tick . . . flap
Beware when buying an eagleotch.
It looks like a pocket watch with a picture of an eagle on it,
But when you get home,
It will sprout wings.
It will try to fly back to the shop,
To be sold again,
Which is what the shopkeeper tells it to do
So he gets more money.
So don't blame me if you see someone with your . . .
Eagleotch!

Michael Paget (12)
Thomas Keble School, Stroud

A House In High Field Road

Big as the school's hall
My garden is as big as the school field
My bedroom is as small as a cupboard
The house is as big as a king's house
My mum's room is as big as a lorry
My sister is as grumpy as a pig
My dog is as big as an elephant.

Jonathon Sharp (11)
Thomas Keble School, Stroud

The Tynings

You're beautiful
You smell like socks
You're lovely
The dog is cuddly
My bedroom is small and cosy
Our living room is nicely decorated like a rich person's
Mum's room is the size of an elephant.

Bradley Sargent (11)
Thomas Keble School, Stroud

The Businessman And The Tramp

In the tube station,
8.30 Kings Cross station.
A heap of rugs,
With a tramp among them,
Sat on the floor,
Staring up at an elegant, rich businessman,
Holding a beautiful woman's hand.

The businessman,
In a fine three-piece suit,
With the beautiful woman,
In a short shirt and black blouse,
With long, soft legs,
On the way to the office.

While the tramp,
A mobile sewage plant,
With legs as hard as steel
And clothes as big as an elephant,
Just starting his day begging.

Gareth Frost (14)
Thomas Keble School, Stroud

A House In Albert Road!

Looks like a pigsty
Smells like cookies baking
Is as little as an ant
Has a barking dog at the door as if he is a roaring tiger
Is as skinny as a rake
Is a bomb that is going to explode
Smells like a wet dog
Is as noisy as a jungle!

Katie Stephens (11)
Thomas Keble School, Stroud

A Sweet Whistle

She whistled like a songbird
And how I loved the sound,
A whistle was new, fed up with words,
I asked her how it was found.

My friend hadn't got the time,
Foolishly, six years old:
'You show me how!' I whined,
'If so you'll have my dog,' I told.

Went home and informed my mum,
She was annoyed; I fell down to the floor,
I cried about the thing I'd done,
I could not take it anymore.

Mum you teach me how,
Hours of trying, I made a high-pitched sound,
Yippee! I could do it, oh wow!
I was as proud as a king being awarded his crown.

But it wasn't long before happiness turned to sadness,
I found out whistling wasn't all that great,
But at least that jealousy had gone along with the stress,
Of losing my dog, which I now know, wasn't my fate.

Lucy Stanford (14)
Thomas Keble School, Stroud

My House

My house is like a pile of marshmallows
My house is like 20,000 bricks being built 500 feet high
My house has a PS2 in
It sits there waiting like a cabbage rotting
My kitchen is as small as a Mini Cooper
My living room is as big as two Mercedes cars
My living room is as old as my gramp
My house smells like my family
My blanket is as soft as a bear rug
My bed is as important as my life.

Nathan Huggins (11)
Thomas Keble School, Stroud

Aston Down

As white as a cloud on a rainy day
As long as a whale
Fireplace is as shiny as a new penny
Sitting room is as yellow as the glowing sun
My room is as purple as lilac lavender
My bed is as big as an Olympic swimming pool
Smells like warm cushions
Kitchen worktops are as blue as the ocean.

Isobel Percival (11)
Thomas Keble School, Stroud

A House In Robin Close

My bedroom is as pink as a pig
And my kitchen is as orange as an orange
Our bathroom is as blue as a whale
My mum's room is as brown as chocolate
And our hallway is as yellow as a bee
Our ceilings are as white as snow
Our house is as big as a zoo
With a massive garden
A trampoline and a swimming pool.

Gemma Werrett (11)
Thomas Keble School, Stroud

Vine Cottage

When you come in the door
It smells like a fire has just erupted
When you walk up the stairs
You feel like you are going to fall
When you walk into my room
You think that a bomb's exploded
When you look in the garden
You smell the beautiful summer's day.

Jemima Radmore (11)
Thomas Keble School, Stroud

My Grandad

My grandad's number one!
Grandad is like a cuddly bear
Who cuddles me like a giant teddy

He's like a giant polar bear
Who doesn't growl anymore
I can still taste his beef casserole
And he always had a chocolate drawer

I remember having to shout at him
Because he was so deaf
When he fell asleep
His false teeth used to fall out.

He snores like a grizzly bear growling
He was like a young man becoming old too soon.

My grandad's number one!

Annie Hobbins (11)
Thomas Keble School, Stroud

A Perfect Storm

Waves swirl as the sky is turning,
Te thunder roars and cracking lightning,
Wind in my ears, so worrying and screaming,
The perfect storm coming, approaching,
People running, hiding from the fierce shouting,
Deep blue is the sky, slowly blackening,
In my house I feel in hiding,
From the storm so terrifying,
On this night that Hell with be unleashing,
On this night that the sky will be attacking,
On this night, the perfect storm approaching.

Lara Crook (14)
Thomas Keble School, Stroud

The Storm

Crash! Crash! The wind against my window,
Cold, sheeting rain, the hammering silence chills to the bone,
Rumbles of thunder, flashes of light,
Wailing wind whistles through the trees,
Yelling and running and crashing and screaming, we shiver,
Up on the roof, water all around, dirty and dark and cold,
Swirling below, erasing all in its path, they cry,
All are lost, many alone, shivering drowned rats up on the roofs,
The rain weeps for the dead and the living alike, death all around,
Choking, smothering, as the planes of Hell,
Silent pain screams in their heads,
Dirt, dark and cold all around, fear and sadness, loss and gain,
Whispering darkness, the main storm has passed
But all fight the dawn for it will begin again,
Shivering terror ('Where will we go? What will we do?' they ask)
People struggle out of their attics, home is now a bitter place,
The world has bitten back.

Emma Freeman (14)
Thomas Keble School, Stroud

The Midnight Storm

(Based on 'Patrolling Barnegat' by Walt Whitman)

Crash, crash, the waves and the wild storm raging,
Terrified, petrified people's screams mix with the storm's howling,
Thunder rumbling like the Devil's gleeful laughter,
Waves, water spitting like an angry cat hissing,
Midnight moonlight casting an eerie spell bewitching,
The fog and mist and hellish darkness and dense fog swirling,
Through the murk and gloom mysterious shapes forming,
(Is that a boat or our last hope of any rescue coming?)
Still at dawn the roaring, rushing stops, calmly, quieting
The sky breaks to bright blue, sun shining, sea softly shimmering,
Relief and happiness return, until next time . . .

Clare Fickling (14)
Thomas Keble School, Stroud

My Sister!

She is a howling wolf when she sings
She's my sister
She likes to hit and punch me like a boxer
She's my sister
She is stylish, sassy, stroppy
She's my sister
She spends hours on her hair and likes to pull mine
She's my sister
She's a thief as she enters my room and steals my possessions
She's my sister
She lives in a pigsty and smells like one too
She's my sister
She listens to loud music on full blast as the whole house shakes
She's my sister
She loves me and cares for me, she's great
She's my sister
She's the best, she's always there for me
I love her
She's my sister
But don't tell her that!
She's my sister!

Jessica Girdwood (11)
Thomas Keble School, Stroud

Tamecube

If you walk into the jungle you will see a tamecube
The only one in the world and it will roar!

Don't touch it
This tamecube will bite you:
It likes the person who buys it!

They are dangerous
But if you have it they are so cool
If you say roar, it will
It listens to you!

Josh Chambers (12)
Thomas Keble School, Stroud

War Poem

The sound of bombs
The sound of guns
The sound of screaming
The sound of shouting.

I can see people
I can see the dead
I can see the wounded
I can see their blood.

I smell rotting flesh
I smell tobacco from
The frightened men.

I taste food
Rotten food.

I touch guns
I touch dead friends.

Chris Lees (14)
Thomas Keble School, Stroud

Down View

Smells like smoke
Is a nuts house
Is a small house
Dad is bald
Cat is jumpy
House is cramped
Dog is crazy
Garden is small
Bedroom big as a barn
Sitting room as cold as ice.

Luke Cameron (11)
Thomas Keble School, Stroud

New Orleans

The wind is like a burglar because it takes things away from people
The water is like poison and venom
Bodies are like big, rotten balloons
The wind is like an elephant
Storming through towns and villages
Leaves traces behind it
Mothers are screaming for their children
Babies shifted off without their mothers to a different state
The tornado is like a whirlpool
Houses look like they have been smashed up
The deadly water is full of pollution and sewage
People desperately need food and drink
Very angry people
Wanting help

Can you help?

Stella Watts (15)
Thomas Keble School, Stroud

The Old Cottage

Four hundred and twenty-nine years old
Three bedrooms
One ghost
The house is going to be 430 years old
The kitchen smells of freshly cooked beef
It has lots of features like a big fireplace
The dirty chimney is full of soot and peat
The stone walls are as cold as ice
The floor is as slippery as snow
The walls are as rough as stone.

Josh Preece (11)
Thomas Keble School, Stroud

My Sister's Bedroom

When you enter my sister's room
First, what do you see?
Well, when I go in, I fear my doom
It has cats everywhere, it makes me want to flee.

She has my old bed, my cabin bed
Onto which everything is crammed
I loved that bed but I always bashed my head!
She rules the roost over her bedroom land.

She even has a sofa bed
But it is full of fluffy toys
That has always made me see red
She has the biggest room and to me it always annoys.

Surely you have to see
What her room has done to me!

Sam Westerby (13)
Thomas Keble School, Stroud

A House In Glen Park Crescent

Like a queen's house
Beautiful as a flower
It is a big house
I have two dogs, one cat and lots of fish
My house is like a gorilla
It is like a swimming pool
It is like a forest
It has three bedrooms
Mine is the biggest
My brother's is the smallest.

Chris Evans (11)
Thomas Keble School, Stroud

Dreams

Drifting off into a fairy-tale land,
You can ride a dolphin up to the sun,
Or swim in purple sea with scarlet sand,
Where the sea lions play and unicorns run.
Fairies flitting from flower to flower,
The bluebirds singing a sweet lullaby,
Dandelion clocks telling the hour,
As forty-two winged rusty keys fly by.
Electric-blue trees standing in the crowds
And silver starlight shining in the night,
Jade-green waterfalls crashing through the clouds
With the gold moon out, it's a gorgeous sight.
Night-time messages we all like to keep,
Dreams are like diamonds; precious gems of sleep.

Lizzie Warner (13)
Thomas Keble School, Stroud

A House In Stone Cote Ridge

My house is as snug as a bug in a rug
My bedroom is as cool as the North Pole
My hall is as yellow as the sun
My bathroom is as blue as the sea
My living room is as big as an elephant
My sister's bedroom is as small as a book
One of my bathrooms is as cream as my living room curtains
My family is as nice as pie
I love my house as much as I love ice cream.

Shauney Gobey (11)
Thomas Keble School, Stroud

My Sonnet

A long time has passed and we are now one,
Our love is still growing stronger each day,
My heart is glad for the things we have done
And all of the things that we have to say.
I wish these feelings could last forever,
But one day we may have to part for good,
Though in our hearts we can stay together,
For better or for worse, like lovers should.
I will never forget the times we shared,
Things like these will never, ever leave me,
Mainly because I am sure we both cared,
But we have to let the course of life be.
Deep down inside, I will never regret,
This love we share, I will never forget.

Kelsey Ross (13)
Thomas Keble School, Stroud

Sage Croft

My house is like a giant mushroom
My house is as small as a Nissan Skyline
My house is as bright as the sun
My house is as warm as a duvet
My house is as clean as the moon
My room is like a scrapyard
My house smells like wood
My house is in the middle of nowhere
My house has three TVs.

Jack Gardiner (11)
Thomas Keble School, Stroud

What To Call A Doberman

Food eater
Fat baller
Proud saunter
Fast catcher
Fast protector
Killer guard dog
Annoying stranger
Sharp teether
Black baller
Cat catcher
Food eater
Canis lupus.

Ben Dowdeswell (12)
Thomas Keble School, Stroud

What To Call A Cat

Flea bag
Speed jumper
Fun player
Tree lover
Fast eater
Bright eyes
Loud purring
Mouse hunter
Claw extender
Heavy sleeper
Bird trapper
Big bouncer
Felis.

Tom Woodward (12)
Thomas Keble School, Stroud

What To Call A Croc

Rolling thief
Sly and spy
Fast catcher
Sinking teeth
Bulging eyes
Dripping blood
Sneaky snatcher
Silent violent
Speedy swayer
Human killer
Sand slipper
Dust maker
Sleep lover
Bank climber
Rock faller
Killer lover
Whole swallower
Scaring daring
Boat wrecker
Night hunter
Humpy back
Meal smeller
Claw sharpener
River hunter
Bank sleeper
Egg layer
Bush green
Army brown
Cage hater
Grass cutter
Slippery slider
Human hater
Dawn lover
Super smeller
Mississipiensis.

Oliver Bruce (12)
Thomas Keble School, Stroud

My Sister

She loves her hair more than anything -
Washing it all the time.

When she snores, she is like a pig
Curled up in her pink covers.

She changes her boyfriends every five minutes
Or do they change her?

Her bedroom is a pink dungeon
No one dares to go in.

She always plays her music full blast
She only does it 'cause she knows I don't like it.

But I love her - my sister!

Sophie Townsend (11)
Thomas Keble School, Stroud

My Younger Brother

I love him *but* here are some reasons
Why he is annoying and sweet!
He pushes buttons on the keyboard,
Whilst I am playing on the computer,
But he also asks me if I want anything to eat or drink.
He stands in front of the TV and turns it off,
But he is always ready to play with me.
If I don't play with him, he whinges at me,
He listens to music loudly when he goes to sleep,
When I am playing with my friends in my bedroom
He tries to get through the door,
But I love him and he is part of my family.
My brother!

Molly Harris (11)
Thomas Keble School, Stroud

Pumpwood

My house is a protected tortoise sheltered in a tree
My garden is as green as apple juice
My house is as warm as the sun
My room is blue like the sea
My house is a giant toaster
My bed is as soft as a polar bear
My house is as old as time itself
My family is as big as the planets circulating around me
My house is as loud as a vacuum cleaner.

Michael Doolin (11)
Thomas Keble School, Stroud

A House In Dallaway

My house is as big as an elephant
My favourite thing is my PlayStation 2
I like everything about my house
My house smells like curry
My house has three TVs
My house in the winter is as warm as a slice of toast
My house in the summer is as cool as ice
My house has one computer
My house has six stereos.

Thomas Plaskitt (11)
Thomas Keble School, Stroud

New Orleans

The wind and water covers the town
Like a giant spider's web
People are thrown on the side like rotten fruit
Houses are crumpled like matchbox houses
Cars piled up like toys on the floor
Wind howls through the town like a pack of wolves
The wind throws people around like litter on the street.

Michael Hayward-Berry (15)
Thomas Keble School, Stroud

Hallowe'en

Hallowe'en is the scariest year
Where people scream
At the ghostly ghosts.

Children shout all night
To get their treats
If they don't get what they want
Then they'll do a trick
That swoops them off their feet.

When the night gets too late
All the children go to bed
Then they are fast asleep
In their nice warm beds
Instead of in the ice black cold
Where it's cold.

All children love Hallowe'en
So they can eat their treats.

Jade Humphries (14)
Thomas Keble School, Stroud

Hurricane Katrina

The water is like venom,
The wind is bellowing.
The greedy water steals houses,
The water is like a murderer.
The rip, twirling wind is like the Devil torturing people
The hurricane is like a black panther killing someone.
The wind bites like a tiger,
The hurricane sucks you up
And swallows you whole.
The waves are shattering,
Houses squashed and flattened,
Families destroyed,
The wind steals people's lives.

Michael McClung (15)
Thomas Keble School, Stroud

A Lot Has Changed

Not as many signs at the beaches or pubs
Now we can walk across the shore
And have a drink with different people.

No more eating bunny chows
But not yet eating haute cuisine.

No more wishing they'll let me in
Eyes glaring through the pub window
With my mouth as dry as a desert.

But there are still signs up here and there:
'Do not pass - whites only'
Splitting us up into two sections,
Like there are sides.

But a lot has changed.

Tyrell Edmond (14)
Thomas Keble School, Stroud

My Cat

Her eyes are like jewels that shine in the dark
Her whiskers are like bristles on a brush
Her claws are as sharp as a knife
Her tail is like a snake wriggling in the grass.

Her patches of fur are like the leaves in autumn
When she chases spiders she squeaks like a mouse
She sleeps on her back and her paws cover her eyes
From the bright lights
She roams the garden like a lion in the jungle
My cat, I love her to bits.

Luke Dyer (11)
Thomas Keble School, Stroud

My Morning

Morning
And Sam wakes up
The sound of birds
Chirping in his ear
As they start to fade away into the distance.

Pet dogs
And neighbours picking up their papers
The sun shining brightly
From up above
Outside Sam's back garden.

Come back to bed
The warm duvet cover
And the soft pillow calling.

Asleep again,
Asleep again.

Sam Reeves (14)
Thomas Keble School, Stroud

My Dog, Meka

My dog, Meka was a black and white husky
That howled at the moon on the darkest night.

Meka was as strong as an ox
Able to knock you over when she jumped.

She was a member of the family
She was my best friend
Always there when I needed her.

Meka was like a panda
Who walked us and not we her.

She is gone
But she will always be with me.

Guy Ridgway (11)
Thomas Keble School, Stroud

My Stepmum And Dad

They are getting married in three days,
Like a queen and king counting down the days.

Carrie can cook well for us and our friends,
She is like a chef in a kitchen, there all day.

My dad is tall,
Like a giraffe looking at everything all day.

They both love us
Like we're a pack of lions.

He has a good sense of humour
Like a hyena always laughing.

She loves to play fight
Like a pair of lions playing.

He has a lush truck
That's like a big black dot on wheels.

She is pretty and has short hair
It's like a cat being loved.

He can make our friends laugh
Like a clown in disguise.

Carrie will get clothes
That will make our friends go, 'Wow!'

They are the best people in the world
Like diamonds and gold.

Cherrie-Jade Harrison (11)
Thomas Keble School, Stroud

My Poem

Hurricanes come and hurricanes go,
Nothing prepares you for such a blow.
Katrina is her name,
Devastation is her game.
This is God's doing,
Now the place is a ruin.
Innocent lives are lost in this disaster,
They should rename it Master Blaster.
The roads are empty, shops are shut,
What can we do to clean things up?
Evacuation is the only way out,
We have no choice, without a doubt.
When we come back in the army bus,
Let's hope you will pray for us.

Amy Bloomfield (13)
Thomas Keble School, Stroud

Audley House

Eight hundred and forty-seven years old
Occupied by an evil goblin
My house is as big as a mountain
The smell in my kitchen is like many fruits all mixed together
The living room stinks of fish food because of the fishes
My room's colour is as green as grass
My attic is a dust ball
There's a stench of cleaner in the bathroom
The garden is a field full of exciting things to do
My floor is as slippery as ice
The walls are as hard as rock.

James Patrick McElroy (11)
Thomas Keble School, Stroud

The Beam

The beam; an obstacle that craves great poise,
Heart ablaze with fear but mind rich with hope,
She starts: focused and ready, she hears no noise,
With leaps and bounds, her nerves tighten like rope.
Her strength and skill displayed gracefully with ease,
Energy flows through her as she performs a flip:
Beautifully arching her back and bending her knees,
She flicks up her legs then back down they whip.
One step, then two, her heart skipping a beat,
The gymnast prepares, breathes and with elegance,
She spins through the air, her arms straight and neat,
Then returns to the beam, steadying her balance.
As she twists and twirls, landing gently on the floor,
The judges below begin deciding her score.

Katharine Birkin (13)
Thomas Keble School, Stroud

War Poem

People dying
People lying on the floor like autumn leaves
Gasses spreading like mist on a cold winter morning
Shells exploding
Soldiers trying to fight the war away
Soldiers rotting away and rats nibbling on dead bodies
Wet and soggy trenches
Horrible tinned war food
Bombs blowing up cities and civilisation
Nobody there to care.

Pete Morgan (14)
Thomas Keble School, Stroud

Untitled

As we sit and stare watching days go by
Like birds we too will find our wings and fly
Fly on through whatever life throws our way
We secretly dream of what we will say
We live through our lives with hope and fear
Within each rainbow you find a tear
Of a child that suffers and pays the price
Only God holds the key and throws the dice
Lies only hide what is true to your heart
Best friends stay forever but love may part
Love is always there yet we do not know
We follow our path and let our love grow
We make mistakes but learn from every one
Things in the past have already been done.

Katie Shaylor (13)
Thomas Keble School, Stroud

Alone In The Dark

It was dark
And I was alone,
A shell went off and I was deafened.
I could not hear,
People were screaming,
But I could not help.
Then all you heard was a *bang!*
My mate had been shot,
I tried not to cry,
But I did.

Kimberley Anne Cole (14)
Thomas Keble School, Stroud

The Great Destruction

The sound is loud
The sound is deafening
The sound you can hardly hear
The sound is a sudden silence
The sound of a sudden bomb exploding.

The sight of dead bodies
The sight of destruction
The sight I can't believe
The sight of Germans
The sight of my mate exploding.

The smell of the gas
The smell of cigarette smoke
The smell of dead bodies rotting
The smell of the medical drugs
The smell of pollution in the air.

The taste of the food
The taste of some gas
The taste of sick as it's running up my throat
The taste I really hate
The taste, there is no taste.

I touch my gun
I touch my friend
I touch the dead bodies in disbelief
I touch my food
I touch everything.

Michael Ryan (14)
Thomas Keble School, Stroud

Remember Me

My soul is released
From the small prison
That was my body
Do not mourn at this spot
For I am free

I am the wind whistling
Through your hair
The breeze that hugs you
As you speed down the hill

Do not fear the danger
Or the dirt jumps and the skidding rocks
For I will be the thick tyres
That speed you along

In every splash of mud
In every blade of grass
That brushes by
My spirit lives on.

Ben Free (12)
Thomas Keble School, Stroud

Everything's Changed

When I walk down and look left and right
My head spins like a wheel on a bike
I'm panicking breathing like a panting dog
I want to go in
I want it to be the way it was
They look at me as if I don't belong
I feel like a red pin in a box of white
Why does it have to be this way?
Can't we all get along?
Can't we all be friends?

Lisa Brazneill (14)
Thomas Keble School, Stroud

Greed Misleads

Our perfect artwork, by strong, talented artists,
Our well laid out gardens with marble arches
And handmade stone fountains.
Our little English tea rooms that pay tribute
To our well-cultured and civilised society,
Our perfect lawns, for croquet we play, good manners to all,
Ensure not to offend.
Our manor houses open to all, that look great all year round,
Especially in fall,
While we smile and give warm welcomes.

A child dies
Every three seconds
In Africa!

Rachel Bentall (15)
Thomas Keble School, Stroud

The Best Day Ever!

My stomach was a thundering earthquake
My heart was a galloping horse
My knees were a shaking tambourine
My teeth were chattering
Our words flowed endlessly
Number exchanged quickly
Our faces touched
It was an electric shock of happiness
Our tongues twisted and turned vigorously
It felt magical
I knew it was right
It went together like salt and pepper
Wow! It was amazing!

Rachel Montague (14)
Thomas Keble School, Stroud

The Beggar And The Shopper

The beggar sits in the cold, dark alleyway;
Staring out and watching people go past him,
Not taking the slightest bit of notice that he's there,
His torn, scrappy look, looks like an old mop,
His slick, dark-grey hair sticks to his face
And his head like glue.

The shopper's straight, light-brown shoulder length hair,
Flies about in the wind as she is walking,
She is weighed down by brand name shopping bags,
She is wearing a knee-length black skirt,
With an ironed black jacket,
Her shiny black shoes still look as good as new,
Her phone rings, she gets it out and she is talking
And wandering around as she is chatting.

Then a deep black convertible,
Comes speeding around the corner,
A man gets out of it and grabs her bags,
She climbs elegantly into the car,
The man is wearing a dark blue suit,
With a neatly tied tie and shiny, dark shoes.

Sophie Ryan (14)
Thomas Keble School, Stroud

Nothing's Changed

Roaring kids, squawking adults
Abuse flying everywhere
Nothing's changed
Same old story, heard it all before
She said that and he did this
The gulf grows city like
As the police turn up
Sirens screaming, children bleeding
Nothing's changed.

Danie Russell (14)
Thomas Keble School, Stroud

That Kid Who Always Gets Spoilt

I slouch there staring at a kid in the clothes shop,
My dismal £20 money that I painstakingly saved,
It's slaves pay for babysitting a little monster!
I stride to the sale rack and browse for a pair of trousers,
£10 the cheapest!
Great, this shop is a rip-off!
I glare back at that kid screeching at her mom,
'But Mom, I've only had £50 spent on me!'
I detest the way those kids behave!

You can tell by her clothes she was spoilt!
Stylish boots that must have cost a bomb,
Pink top embroidered with gold patterns,
Her skirt - that folded style I've always loved!
Her golden locks which she swayed as she barked,
Her make-up visible even at such a young age.

She stares back at me,
'Look at what that girl's wearing, Mom!'
I stare back, my eyes about to pop out,
I look down at what I'm wearing -
A jet-black vest and punk-style jeans.

She stares at a bag and instructs her mom to buy it,
£60, my parents wouldn't even consider it.
Her mom hands over the Switch to the women at the desk,
Her daughter, now angelic has a grin on her face,
Then they're gone, just like that.

I come out of my dream of being one of them
And enter the nightmare of the real world.

Kerry Stephens (14)
Thomas Keble School, Stroud

What If?

What if I get caught stealing these sweets?
After all, they are only sweets, just a few penny sweets,
Nothing much!
What if I get caught taking this money?
I know I shouldn't,
But it's only a quid!
No one will miss it,
It's just a quid!
What if I get caught stealing this car?
I just want to take it for a joyride,
Only a spin around the block,
I'll put it back, honest!

But then . . .
What if I get caught breaking into this house?
Take a few bits, sweets, money and a bit of jewellery,
Surely that's worth quite a bit
And it comes to the car!
Ah yes, the car.
The fun of it all,
Only a battered old GTi,
Only worth a few grand,
Just a couple of grand!

So it started with sweets, then the money,
But it always, always gets worse,
It then went to cars, computers, even more,
Now I'm sitting here thinking . . .
Should I have taken those sweets?
Should I have taken that money?
And that GTi, now that was a mistake!

So I think next time, I will say no,
It's wrong
And that's that!

Just say no!

Rachel Bedford (14)
Thomas Keble School, Stroud

Dancing

A pirouette and strong, proud arabesque,
The tap of feet and swish of silk by night,
The beat of drums and twirl of bodies slight,
Plucking of harps tells tales of happiness,
The stars are the jewels on her fine dress.
Music leaps out at you, like birds from nest,
Dance like a citrus fruit with all its zest,
Purity can be found in ballet pure.
In flamenco the click of castanets,
In a French nightclub the cancan started,
On stage the dancers bowed, then they darted.
Sweet country dancers swing around the hall,
Flowing dresses sweep the floor at the ball,
We did one final dance and then parted.

Jemma Lewis (14)
Thomas Keble School, Stroud

Down By The Lake

The sun is warm and shining strong,
The lake is a sparkling calm,
Trees are growing tall and long,
Gazing at the distant farm;
I see horses running wild,
With their white manes flowing free,
Below my feet the fishes three;
Are swimming hand in fin,
I sit and stare down at the blue,
As if it were a sin,
The ripples running through,
I dip my feet into the blue
And as I do, I wait for you.

Amanda Engstrom (13)
Thomas Keble School, Stroud

Friends!

Throughout my life my friends have come and gone,
Sometimes they have stood by me all my life,
Some have been inspirations and have shone,
With some friends we have been like man and wife,
Some have been idols, some have been heroes,
Some friends say I'm bad, some say I am good,
Friends I have lots of, enemies come to zero,
I would fly for my friends if I could!
I don't like people who talk behind me,
I try not to be mean to anyone,
Physical violence is never the key,
I try to keep all of my friends number one,
Always stick with your friends, believe me now,
To have lots of friends, be kind, that is how!

Megan Baker (13)
Thomas Keble School, Stroud

Enchantment

The tiny faeries by the wishing well
The mystic pixies by the waterfall
See elves in cracks of a crumbling brick wall
Enchanted creatures in a wooded dell
The bright flowers and their hypnotic smell
Listen hard to hear their delicate call
Open your mind and eyes wide to see all
Each one made as small specks of stardust fell
On a summer's morning among the dew
Or as a rainbow appears in the sky
You'll see the precious figures as they fly
And that memory will be special to you
Perhaps you'll wonder if it's really true
When each reflection glistens in your eye.

Isabelle Starkiss (13)
Thomas Keble School, Stroud

Equality

Whether you are queuing for a bus,
Sitting down on the seats,
Or actually getting off the bus

Whether you are playing football with your friends,
Watching it on the box with your family,
Or buying the new kit

Whether you are sitting on a bench,
Eating your lunch on it,
Or just watching the people around you . . .

Black or white
Towering or matchbox height
Grotesque or picture perfect

Whatever you are, whatever you do,
Equality should be a right for everyone.

Rachel Rendell (15)
Thomas Keble School, Stroud

Cricket

I cannot show my passion for matches,
Cricket is my favourite sport,
I cannot show my feeling for catches,
Cricket battles have been fought,
I am a bat getting battered,
Cricket bat made out of willow,
Even though it doesn't matter,
I think of cricket asleep on my pillow,
Hitting a six or being bowled,
LBW, bad light stops play,
I am a fielder getting cold,
Play will continue another day.

Sam Mincher (12)
Thomas Keble School, Stroud

Sun

The sun is shining but
Struggling to stay bright
The clouds start to darken
But no!
The sun reappears and takes over the sky
The birds are singing
The bees are humming
Then suddenly
Crash!
The rain comes tumbling down
Lighting flashing
Street lights wondering whether to stay on or off
Thunder crashing!
Then just like that
The sun comes out from nowhere
And the sun rules the sky once
Again!

Anika Ponting (12)
Thomas Keble School, Stroud

Think Of Me When I'm Gone

Don't think of me in a hole underground
Think of me as the twang of the guitar
Think of me as an active background dancer
Think of me as a harmonious singer singing beautifully
Think of the hard work you put into the guitar
Think of me as the practise you put into
Playing the guitar
Dancing the night away
Singing most gracefully
So don't think of me in a hole
Think of this poem as me.

Nadine Marks (12)
Thomas Keble School, Stroud

My Life As A Dance . . .

I have not gone,
I must carry on.
I am a short, sharp dance move,
Always in the groove!
I am a heartbeat never stopping,
Even when I'm body popping!
I am a move scoring points,
Usually using all of my joints.
I am a costume worn in a show,
Just remember that I will go.
I am a glint in a disco ball,
I will always be there to call
Your name when I'm feeling low,
Always, always come to my show!
I have not gone,
I must carry on . . .

Kayleigh Louise Adams (12)
Thomas Keble School, Stroud

Horse Riding

H orse's young playing in the morning
O btaining the highest jump at the show
R iding on a summer's night watching the sunset
S how jump with the rain running off my nose
E quine beauty glistening in the sun

R ough ground hitting the horse's back when it rolls
I am the sound of the horse's hooves hitting the ground
D ragging the feed bag back to the food room
I am the calmness of the horse's heart
N aughty horses bucking people off
G rabbing the saddle quickly before we go.

Roberta Wilkes (12)
Thomas Keble School, Stroud

Terrorism And War

Terrorism and war
It affects us all
    Is there any point
    In this needless violence?
        America, Iraq, even England
        Is there any point
            In this needless massacre?
            Guns 'n' ammo
                Bombs 'n' explosives
                Is there any point
                    In this needless destruction?
                    Planned attacks
                        In significant places
                        This needs to stop
                          Now!

Paul Stephens (15)
Thomas Keble School, Stroud

Do Not Cry For Me, My Family

Don't cry for me, my family
The truth is I never left you;
I am the voices of angels blown in the wind.
I am the perfectly tuned voices,
Waiting to rejoice in my life at my funeral.
I am the wonderfully composed anthem,
Ready to be sung with enthusiasm.
I am the peaceful cathedral, known to everyone,
Clean and interesting waiting to be visited.
Don't cry for me, my family,
The truth is, I will *never leave your side.*

Hannah Rachel Bucknell (12)
Thomas Keble School, Stroud

Man's So-Called Friend . . .

Man's so-called friend,
    And the trusty track.
Pushing the pedals,
    No turning back.
Heat of the summer,
    Cool inside.
Now the summer's over
    And so is the ride.
Prices are soaring,
    So bring out your bike.
No fuel left now,
    They're going on strike.
So take to the pavement,
    Walk down the street.
Overcrowded sidewalk,
    There's traffic on feet.
And take to the trains,
    The planes and the bus.
They've always been there,
    So what is the fuss?
But friends become foes,
    As you already know.
So start to use your feet,
    Because your car will not go.

Ed Bryant (15)
Thomas Keble School, Stroud

Selfish Personality

One old fat man
One old dog
One old fat TV
And a selfish personality

The old fat man sits on his throne
Sipping his delicate tea
Watching those not as fat as he,
As they struggle their way through reality

One old fat man
One old dog
Leaving tiny scraps for one
A tiny bounty for another

The old fat man sits on his throne
Eating his fattening cakes
He feels no hunger yet he still eats,
His stomach is fully complete

All our stomachs are fully complete
Yet still we feel compelled to eat
We think not of those living elsewhere
Starving to death as we speak

Everyone says something must be done,
So why are we still sitting at home
Like the old man sitting on his throne,
The old fat man and his dog in his home?

Sophie Dennis (15)
Thomas Keble School, Stroud

Marriage And Divorce

Isn't it special on your wedding day?
You love
Honour
And obey
It's meant to be the happiest day of your life
Sharing it with someone you truly love
In sickness and in health
All the presents
Fun
And family around
What more could anyone want
Or ask for?
The rest of your life maps out ahead
The days turn to months
The months turn to years
Yet all the time you're living in bliss, happily married
Or so you think

Till death us do part?
Isn't that what it's mean to be?
Yet half of England ends up
Divorced.

Katie Ponting (15)
Thomas Keble School, Stroud

A Final Palette Of Black

A final palette of black,
An epidemic with no cure,
A blissful silence.
As their bleeding souls lay in the fallen leaves of autumn,
They experienced tears with no pain,
All is gone,
All is forgotten,
Inherit my memories.

Becci Jennings (15)
Thomas Keble School, Stroud

Foreign England Football Manager

Isn't international football meant to be
About the nation coming together?
Not about a balding Swede.

The England team should display
Passion
Skill
And take on the nation's dreams
Yet this is ruined by an outsider.

This alien manager cares more about
His designer suits
Female colleagues
And wage packet
Than about winning.

The nation waits in anticipation
Is it our turn to win it this time?
Surely we can beat this opposition?

No

Players being played out of position
Formations with strange new names
The celebrity players bossing their boss
Who, just sits, watching the defeat
With an expressionless face.

The nation's hopes and dreams
Are lost on this outsider
When will an English manager return
To the throne meant for no foreigner.

This clueless Swede
Has destroyed a proud footballing nation
Leaving its fans heartbroken and ridiculed.

But for him, this is mission accomplished.

Jamie Ponting (15)
Thomas Keble School, Stroud

The Sticky Labels On Milk Bottles

Don't talk to me about war,
Don't talk to me about religion
And don't even think about talking to me about politics.

Some people get annoyed about bullying,
Some people get annoyed about democracy,
But I'll tell you what annoys me . . .
Sticky labels on milk bottles!

Talk about annoying the public,
Happily sat picking the labels off of the milk bottle
And what do you find?
The label won't come off cleanly,
But to leave a sticky mess around the bottle.

I have to sit there with a sticky mess on my hands;
All I was simply trying to do was take a label off of a bottle.
Is it too much to ask?
Will I have to suffer for much longer,
Or is someone going to realise the problem and take some action?

It would make everyone's life so much easier,
Simple really, but you'd think it's rocket science,
The way it's not being sorted out.

So what I'm saying is . . .
Forget sorting out better school dinners,
Worrying about politics and what's going on in the world,
Worry about having no sticky labels on milk bottles.

I mean, get your priorities right . . .

Kate Melsome (16)
Thomas Keble School, Stroud

England

Welcome to our glorious nation
Where everyone has a say
Where everyone can cast votes
Where we can be proud of our democracy.

We're friends with everyone -
America - best friends
We co-operate with Europe too
Yet, we have always been strong and independent.

We denounce all racism in the rest of the world
All men and women are treated the same
We embrace different cultures and religions
Anyone can be prime minister if they work for it.

We can be proud of our history
We brought an end to the slave trade
We built a beautiful nation and invented
Football, the game that unifies all nations.

We're England!
Why not wake up, look at all we've done
And then see how proud you are.

Robbie Gillett (15)
Thomas Keble School, Stroud

New Orleans

The stars are faded by heavy black clouds,
The only form of light to be seen,
Power lines down,
Food supplies out,
No whites to be sighted,
Bush's society being broken apart,
By colours of skin,
The people of New Orleans,
Left by a freak of nature.

Kate Carpenter (15)
Thomas Keble School, Stroud

Do Not Be Sad That I've Gone!

Do not be sad that I've gone
Remember me through this song

My energy is strong
I am the lyrics in this song
Loud, energetic and long from gone.
Do not be sad that I've gone
Remember me through this song!

I am talent
I am a star
My ambition is living on
So do not be sad that I've gone
Remember me through this song

I write my thoughts down on paper
Don't be afraid to read them later
Do not be sad that I've gone
Remember me through this song!

Sophie Jay Weston (12)
Thomas Keble School, Stroud

Water

Do not be upset when I have gone,
I'll have already come back as something long.
I am flowing, gentle and sometimes calm,
I see lots of oak and sometimes palm.
I never sleep, I never die,
People smile when I go by.
I am all over the place,
I am a river with a pace.
I am a brook all bubbly and bright,
I am a swamp home to animals at night.

Hannah Wynter (12)
Thomas Keble School, Stroud

I Am The Music

Tell everybody not to stand by my gravestone,
All that's there are my old bones.
But I am not there, my spirit is away,
I'll maybe come back some day.
For the while,
Just smile,
Because,
I am the song stuck in your head,
I am not dead,
I am the high notes squealing with new days,
I am here always,
I am the music.

At my funeral don't cry,
I am not gone, don't say goodbye,
Only my body is in the box of sad,
I am happy now, please be glad
And remember,
I have not gone,
I am the words that make you feel you can relate,
I am the tune that decides your fate,
I am the beat that makes you want to sing,
I am the song on the radio that's never boring,
I am the music.

Annie Chaplin (12)
Thomas Keble School, Stroud

Football Crazy

F ootball crazy that's what I am
O h! He's scored a goal
O uch! That's gotta hurt
T op corner, what a goal
B y jove! He's done it again
A nd now I am the ball as it curls past the keeper's hand
L aunched and that ball's away
L ook at that, it's as if he is the ball!

Liam Ballinger (12)
Thomas Keble School, Stroud

Remembered In Metal

I am long H air being flung around
I am the E ar-splitting super fast solos
I am an A coustic chord being picked
I am the V ery guitar so sleek
I am the Y ell of a front man on show

I am the M etal, complete from top to toe
I am an E lectric power source making things work
I am the T wang of a well tuned guitar
I am the A ce fast picking of the bass player
I am the L ight speed drumming of a crazy drummer

Remember me, for all of these things,
It's what I live for,
Or so my soul sings.

Miles Lewis-Iversen (12)
Thomas Keble School, Stroud

Thoughts

I have lots of views
I have lots of thoughts
But how do you put them on paper?
How do you write your feelings?
How can you write them so that everyone understands?
You can't.
Well, I don't think you can
I just can't put it into words.

I guess I should stop trying
I know what I believe
Surely that's enough
You don't need to know as well
I don't want to know your thoughts
And I guess you won't know mine.

Rebecca Starkiss (15)
Thomas Keble School, Stroud

Remember Me

Do not stare at my ashes and cry
I am not there, I didn't die

I am the energy that rushes through your body
I am the dance floor quake
I am the bass of thirty inch speakers
I am the dust in the roof that shakes.

Please don't stare at my ashes and cry
I'm not there, I didn't die
Please have a party of R'n'B
Please have a party just for me.

Please don't forget my ambitions in life
Please don't forget my friends
Please don't forget my life and memories
I am still here, it did not end.

Billie Wiseman (12)
Thomas Keble School, Stroud

I Am

When I pass on,
I am not gone.
I am still here,
Among your peers.
I am still around and carry on,
Carrying on, with what I live for,
I am the dance and moves to the song,
I move around on the dance floor,
I am the smile as you dance your heart away,
I am the excitement as the crowd cheer you on,
I am the music helping you along,
I am the adrenaline as you take to the floor,
When I pass on,
I am not gone,
I am around, still living on.

Jasmine Hicks (12)
Thomas Keble School, Stroud

I Am
(Based on 'Do Not Stand at my Grave and Weep' by Mary Frye)

When I'm gone do not cry or weep
I am not dead, I'm just asleep
I am the song that will hold in your mind
I am the notes on a blackened line
I am the music that is all around
I am the gentle, uplifting sound
When I'm gone, please don't say goodbye
'I am not there, I did not die'.

Hannah Bloomfield (12)
Thomas Keble School, Stroud

Live And Let Die

It is time for me to go,
I must now let my flower grow,
I leave the world a better place,
Only to expand the human race,
I am neither asleep nor awake,
I am not lying there in front of you,
But always watching over you.

Henry Walker (13)
Thomas Keble School, Stroud

Sport

Sport, I am sport,
I am the feeling of winning a gold medal,
Happiness and satisfaction are the feelings of winning.
I am a team tactics man who finds the winning play,
Intelligence in this man's trade, thinking is his game.
I am Paula's pacemaker who runs for fun,
You need determination to go all the way.
So if you need something to do, turn to sport,
Because I'll help you.

Samuel Driscoll (13)
Thomas Keble School, Stroud

Laryngitis

Silence. Why? Nothing to say?
Over 4,000,000 words in the English language
And still nothing to say? Why?
Why not say something?
What is this deadly silence in aid of?
Why not speak your mind?
You sit there in a speechless state of silence,
While others . . .

                        Gabble! Gabble! Gabble!
                              They won't shut up!
                              They can't shut up!
                      Talking to the world at large . . .
                The most random things imaginable
But at least they speak . . .

Still in silence, you watch the crowd,
Chatting and laughing noisily.
Deafening whispers, drifting from the other side of the room,
Meet your ears, as if they were calling out to you . . .
But no,
Nobody will speak to you anymore . . .
You long to reply, talk back to the faceless voices,
The constant buzz of casual chatter tormenting you . . .

If only your silence could be broken . . .

Craig Banyard (15)
Thomas Keble School, Stroud

Black And White

Why does it matter about the colour of our skin?
    Does anyone deserve to be a victim of a racist attack?
If I'm black, so what?
Do I deserve to be punished for being different?

My son took his A Levels,
He made me so proud,
    Who gave you the right to take my baby boy away from me?
        Did you really need to end his life before it really began?
All it took was one blow to the head,
    Just a single one,
Now he's dead.

You're two white boys, with hoods and no hearts,
Spending your time ending innocent lives, in big parks.

Why did you do it?
    Was it because of his skin?

You mixed passed skin colours in a park,
    Did you need to cause such pain and distress?
He never did anything to you,
Just got on with school and life itself,
    But now he's dead,
        From your blow to his head.

So will this happen every time you see black people?
    Or will you control your awful anger?
I'm white, I don't kill,
    So why should you?

Lisa Rice (15)
Thomas Keble School, Stroud

Different Backgrounds

A 40-year-old woman,
Sat at the kitchen table,
Staring at the bills,
Each containing the stamp,
'Final Warning'
There she sits,
Crying,
In the depressing council house,
Sobbing the words repeatedly,
'I cannot pay,'
A letter lays open on the table,
An appointment with the bank manager.

A wealthy, married man,
Sat in his massive study,
Reading emails on his state of the art computer,
One from the bank manager,
Wishing to meet with him today,
To discuss his successful investments.

They both sit in the waiting room,
The man accompanied by his son,
The women sits,
Thinking about the bills,
She is filled with envy,
As she listens to the rich man's son,
Continually asking for toys and money,
Knowing that she can't give that to her children,
She feels worthless,
She wishes for an easy life,
Away from hardships,
Which she constantly battles with,
A nice house in a safe society,
A fancy car,
Designer clothes,
Just like that man has,
She knew he had money,
She'd do anything for that,
Anything!

Josie Fowler (15)
Thomas Keble School, Stroud

Remember Me

Remember me as the autumn leaves sway
Remember me when I have gone away
Remember me not, lying still up there
Skin pale, bleak and cold, dry and bristle hair
Remember me as a person of joy
Me as a girl, you as a little shy boy
Your straight hair golden, my wavy hair brown
We walked hand in hand around the town
Our young faces glowing, our soft lips red
Who would have thought after all we had said
That we would be apart for evermore
God, doesn't life seem such a chore and a bore
Remember me as who should be your friend
With this poem, my soul, angels send.

Leah Pucknell (13)
Thomas Keble School, Stroud

Poem

It's not time to panic when I am dead,
You will still see me sleeping in my bed.
I will go to Heaven not down to Hell,
Think of your wedding with those big church bells.
I plead you not to cry above my grave,
Stick up for yourself just keep being brave.
Please do not start to sob and cry and weep,
Just forget about me and go to sleep.
Remember me for what I always do,
Using the computer, you need it too.
Remember the days when you were happy,
I was wearing that soft cuddly nappy.
You are my mother and I am your son,
So I am still here, so don't be glum.

Jordan Coxhead (13)
Thomas Keble School, Stroud

My Animal Poem

It lies in wait of something
To disturb its everlasting slumber.
The world as we know it
Is getting dumber and dumber.

It's killing off our soldiers
Turning them to ash.
Our greatest leaders
Don't have the weapons or the cash.

Lurks in the night
And stalks in the day.
Even the countries of the world
Haven't anything to say.

No cars, no planes
Just carts and wagons.
Thanks to the dreaded
Sapphire dragon.

Perry Smith (12)
Thomas Keble School, Stroud

Please Remember Me

Do not stand at my grave and cry,
I am an eagle who can fly high.
I'm the grass between dogs' paws
And the willow tree that the cat claws.
I never picked on others,
Nor hit my innocent brothers.
But I am the air in which you all breathe,
Remember, I never wished to leave -
All my family and friends,
But everyone's life has to end.

Emily McCollum (13)
Thomas Keble School, Stroud

The Sandstorm

Screech, screech, screams the wind, sand still high rising,
Miniature marbles pelting into your face,
Viciously scorching marks out of your flesh,
Peering around for any signs of shelter,
But nothing at all but many mirages,
Creating false pits of fresh, blue, pure water,
Dotted carelessly around the horizon,
The cutting wind piercing through, throwing up clumps of sand,
Dispersing them at all irregular angles,
Hours and hours crawl by,
But still the stones keep on lashing around,
The gods up above, smiling to one another,
While I am crouched down,
Every muscle in my body throbbing,
But the storm will go on, as it drifts into the night.

Arthur Milroy (14)
Thomas Keble School, Stroud

Please May I Have:

This is what I would like to achieve
Good money, good job, an actress maybe,
A very big house, a very nice car
A great family who think I'm a star,
I want loads of friends who can have some fun,
A couple of healthy and nice children,
To be able to play guitar really well,
To still be able to laugh and smile,
To be able to run a few miles,
Travel the world to lots of destinations,
To succeed in people's expectations,
Help out and give money to charity
And to stay nice, talented and witty!

Rosie Haighton (13)
Thomas Keble School, Stroud

Portage No. 6

Through the woods - like a horror film - running
Rain lashes slantways, my back is now soaking
This pack wants to drag me to the ground as I'm staggering
Thunder like gunshots suddenly snapping
Then the forest is lit in a blaze of white lightning
Where it hits, just off the path, trees crashing
Somewhere ahead of me, the night is ripped by screaming
Feet slip, the mud path is running
Through the blue/black darkness, on rocks slipping
(Up ahead - a fork - which path to take?
Now I'm saved by someone screaming)
Slammed in the ford by the river fast flowing
The thin trail winds, up the creek, over boulders, always rising
Running off adrenaline for a back-breaking ending
As more thunder cracks the night, never ceasing.

Maya Schunemann (14)
Thomas Keble School, Stroud

The Storm

In it came like waves washing upon the sand,
Spilling over and distorting the land.
Swilling, splashing, it ripped down each street,
Where concrete once was, water at my feet.
The sky once peaceful, now filled with fear,
No place to hide, nothing seems clear.
Hurrying and rushing it took it all,
Not once did it stop nor did it stall.
Dirty brown water from ceiling to floor,
Personal possessions gone, ruined, no more.
Like a monster it came,
People accused and blamed.
That sky once filled with fear, now peaceful again,
Thousands of lives in tatters, thousands of futures unclear.

Stephanie King (14)
Thomas Keble School, Stroud

Disaster On A Street Near You

A quiet, suburban street,
Cool breeze lifting blades of grass,
The sun glaring down on its kingdom,
All is calm, all is still and all is safe.
Suddenly a dog barks, breaking the lazy silence,
The whining continues, desperately, unexpectedly,
The wind picks up its pace to a trot,
Dark shadows sweep over the landscape,
Bringing an icy chill and a distant roaring,
Then a huge shape looms over the buildings,
Twisting and contorting in mindless fury,
Spitting shredded needles at its victims,
Everything spiralling towards this maniacal demon . . .
And then the rage passes over,
A quiet, suburban wasteland,
Save the rising wails of humanity.

Theo Deproost (15)
Thomas Keble School, Stroud

The Hurricane's Consequences

Rush, rush, the foul, sluggish water gushing
Down the urban river, dead bodies flowing
Dogs and cats, howling and hissing
Loudest of all, people screaming
Nobody there, helping the dying
Nobody there, helping the living
So many dead, so many dying
Four days have gone, the army's coming
Five days have gone, people evacuating
Millions of tonnes of water streaming
The weight of tears on a city begging
The weight of death on the living
A city on the brink of dying
A city needing strength to start living.

Jimmy Bower (14)
Thomas Keble School, Stroud

Patrolling New Orleans

Gush, gush, the water, rainwater, flooding
Faces of fear, ever-lasting screaming
Poisonous water has become great tasking
The country's strength is finally showing
It isn't very strong with all these random shootings
They're having trouble with mosquito infestations
Once upon a time it was happy living
Gush, gush, the water, rainwater flooding
Hurricane Katrina was quite surprising
Citizens are not moving
They are now just refusing
Houses are destroyed but lucky to be standing
A terrible time that will be costing
America together is now losing.

Andrew Roberts (14)
Thomas Keble School, Stroud

The Storm Is Brewing

The waves rolling, rolling, turning, tossing,
Crashing up onto the coarse beach,
Dragging the sand relentlessly out to sea,
A storm is brewing concocting like a potion
The salty water crashing downwards
The noise piercing and ringing throughout
The creamy white froth churning
Round and round, up and down
The light from the little lighthouse on the cliff
Beaming out to the smoggy seas
Making the horrific storm even more visible to all spectators
Wrestling winds whipping the water up into the air
Shadowing ships frightfully sailing away from the storm.

Lucy Cole (15)
Thomas Keble School, Stroud

The Door
(Based on 'The Door' by Miroslav Holub)

Go and open the door.

Maybe outside there's
A purple tree that has blossom like a rainbow
Or even a silver rose.

Maybe outside there's
Something you've never seen before
Or another room without another door.

Maybe outside there's
A girl playing on a swim
Or a bird sitting lonely with nothing to sing.

Maybe outside there's
Nothing, everything
Or a normal garden.

Harley-Ray Hill (12)
Thomas Keble School, Stroud

The Phone Call

I lay down on my bed with my ears ringing,
The phone was sounding its alarm,
My dad picked it up with his eyes half open,
He slowly gave the phone to my mum.

She slouched over with her face in her hands,
Tears ran down her cheeks and into her palms,
My brother asked what was wrong,
Silence, not a word.

I went out of the room, then sat down,
My dad said, 'It will be OK,'
Whispers were as silent as a dog whistle,
I didn't say a word.

I didn't want to break the peace and quiet,
My brother and me went,
The house was like a church, so quiet.

Ben Jones (14)
Thomas Keble School, Stroud

The Door
(Based on 'The Door' by Miroslav Holub)

Go and open the door,
Maybe outside there's,
A jungle full of,
Monkeys and bears,
Waiting for their prey.

Go and open the door,
There might be,
A dog house full of fleas,
Where the dogs,
Itch their skin.

Or just maybe,
It's a wardrobe,
Full of all your clothes,
But it could be,
All of your dreams come true!

Sam Sowerby (12)
Thomas Keble School, Stroud

Simply Remember

Don't cry over me, simply remember
The blue sea on the sand in December
The wind whistling through the tall treetops
The blazing sun making you hot
The silence in a class of school children
Remember the place we called a den
The deafening whine of upset horses
The rush of cantering round the best courses
The fluffy white clouds in the clear blue sky
The air so clear so the birds will fly
Remember the big lake at Toadsmoor Woods
I would try to stay with you if I could
Never forget me but always have fun
I will always be with you in your heart and lungs.

Olivia Cole (13)
Thomas Keble School, Stroud

My Accident

I sat all morning in my neighbour's house
Waiting for my mum to arrive
At 3.15 my mum came home

In the door my mum came in
She had had a good day at work
And Sheila saying how wonderful I was

I laughed out loud and saw the door
An open door leading to freedom
I ran out onto the path

I ran straight into the side of a car
My mum and sister had chased me but couldn't reach
A woman driver eh! Typical!

I was rushed to hospital
With small, minor injuries
But just in case, I was kept in overnight.

This time I had cheated *death!*

Adam Loveridge (14)
Thomas Keble School, Stroud

When I'm Gone

When I am gone far far away
Be happy, as happy as can be, trust me
I don't want you to stay out of the way
Please do not go worrying I will be fine
Go out all night and find yourself a life
Honest even if you do cross the line
So please go on my dear, lovable wife
So don't feel guilty if you have a laugh
I don't mind, it's part of a new living
I will be with you, even when you're in the bath
I don't mind if you do a bit of fibbing
I am always with you everyday
So please put your hands together and pray.

Christo Geller (14)
Thomas Keble School, Stroud

So Maybe I'm Not Here Anymore

So maybe I'm not here anymore
I was told that I was bold
Maybe so, but I was old,
But in your mind my soul will seek
A place other than a dirty creek,
So maybe the day has fallen as well,
I shall not trip and go to Hell,
Now sad or happy days are gone
But the family will go on,
Old age is like a cage,
It's taken me but now I'm free,
So maybe I'm not here anymore
I was told that I was bold
Maybe so, but I was old.

Tom Dunn (13)
Thomas Keble School, Stroud

Waiting

My sister and me were waiting for years,
We waited and waited but nothing appeared.

Then suddenly it came out of the blue,
My mum gave in and we went looking.

We knew what we wanted,
The search didn't take long.

As we stood watching,
Searching for one.

Suddenly it waddled over towards us,
My sister picked him up and we took him home.

Yes! It was a cute little puppy
That we named Jasper.

Alistair Raghuram (14)
Thomas Keble School, Stroud

The Break

I stumbled along the road towards my house
Hopping like a pogo stick because my ankle was sore
At 1 o'clock my mum took me to hospital

At the hospital I saw my sister crying
My sister always took injuries to heart
And the doctor said it was a definite fracture

My mum laughed, then said, 'You silly boy!'
When I got back from the hospital I was so embarrassed
I slipped on the floor with my cast and crutches

And my family told me they were sorry for my mishap
Whispers spread saying that I was stupid
For doing it in the first place
My sister was away outside while I lay in bed, I was bored

I moved around in my bed in discomfort
And when my sister got in she said, 'Hi, how you feeling?'
with my leg now bandaged in a bright green cast
I couldn't do anything

Next morning I lay in bed bored out of my mind
And my music playing softly, then my friends came to visit
And signed the cast
It was the fifth week into my six week holiday

I went outside to see my friends
When I saw my friends they gave me 'get well' cards
But when I thought that this was hard my six weeks had passed
I had my injury and still walk today.

Jake Rogers (14)
Thomas Keble School, Stroud

My Memory

It was about five years ago, I was lying in bed resting
As I knew that today was the big day that I got my kitten
I knew that this day would change my life forever.

I had waited for weeks now, for four weeks
For her to be old enough to be taken away from her mum
We were in the car on our way, I was hyper like a monkey
We finally pulled up to the door, my mum parked the car.

We get the cat holder out of the boot of the car
And walk up to the door
We ring the doorbell and wait a minute
The lady answered the door and told us to come in.

I went in and my cat jumped right on me, knowing it was me
We stayed for a bit and talked
About what the cat liked to eat and its diet
We named the cat Pertita because it was the smallest one there.

We got home and let it out, watching it get used to its new home
We left it for five minutes and found the cat had gone,
We started looking and found it behind the TV
Snuggled up, sleeping.

Ryan Ponting (14)
Thomas Keble School, Stroud

Remember Me

Do not weep or cry at my grave, just laugh,
Remember me as the fun guy next door,
I am in the forgotten, grateful land,
I am the next good level you achieve,
Remember me as the fun guy next door,
Do not remember me as impatient,
Do not remember me as horrible,
Remember me as the fun guy next door,
I have achieved what I set out for,
I have achieved all my goals that I set,
Remember me as the fun guy next door.

Jay Newman (13)
Thomas Keble School, Stroud

The Crash

It was a lovely day in the field, the sun was really out,
As I got on the bike, the saddle was hot and burning where I sat,
I let go of the clutch slowly, just to be safe
And then I put the throttle on with the wind in my face.

As I went down the bumps it was really quite a dream,
Going up and down like a wave machine,
I came back round getting ready to stop,
Slowly put the brake on and stopped by my mate, Scott.

We filled the tank without a doubt,
Put on the engine and let it all rip out,
I watched my friend do all the tricks
And all I could do was ride over sticks.

I got back on the bike again,
Thought it would be good,
But all I did was eat some wood,
I put on the throttle speeding away and getting faster as I went.

The wheel came off the ground I was getting quiet scared,
The wheels were turning really fast and I was speeding up,
The tree was getting really close and I knew I was going to crash,
I hit the tree with a bang but I was still OK!

Chris Whitfield (14)
Thomas Keble School, Stroud

Tiger Woods

Number one
Long hitter
Great chipper
Nike sponsor
Immense golfer
Awesome winner
Ball crusher
Ultimate player
Money loaded
Golf dominator.

Tom Organ (13)
Thomas Keble School, Stroud

Everything's Changed

You look away into the deep red sky,
The hot, white, inwards turning of your eyes,
This just lets me know,
Everything's changed.

You used to walk, head held high,
But now hunched back you walk the dirty streets,
This just lets me know,
Everything's changed.

Your thick chestnut hair,
Is now iron grey, dropped low over your eyes,
This just lets me know,
Everything's changed.

How once you used to be,
So smart, so happy
And yet so free to spread your wings and fly,
But now you're
So dirty, so sad, so jailed from life,
This just lets me know,
Everything's changed.

Danielle Girdwood (14)
Thomas Keble School, Stroud

Monkey

Tree climber
Branch hanger
Mad creature
Tail swinger
Fury guy
Cheeky chap
Jungle squeaker.

Emily Nobes (12)
Thomas Keble School, Stroud

The Accident

I sat in the school office all afternoon,
Waiting for my mum to come,
It felt like forever.

At last she came,
I was sat there crying with pain,
We got in the car and went to the hospital.

Still crying, the doctor came,
I had to go for an X-ray,
It was like a big black hole.

The buzzing sound was horrible,
Now I was even more scared,
Again for ages I was waiting.

At last the nurse came,
Another room, but I didn't feel scared,
A yellow plaster was put over my arm.

Six weeks till I was back to normal!

Emma Townsend (14)
Thomas Keble School, Stroud

My Dog

Bone eating
Homework chewing
Dog meeting
(Dog) backside sniffing
Floor sweeper
Annoying creature
My dog.

Alex Hunt (13)
Thomas Keble School, Stroud

The Vet

I sat all alone on the settee,
My mum and dad running in and out,
Trying to get things done.

I sat in silence,
Only thinking about my dog,
Lying in pain in the conservatory.

He'd been in pain for so long,
I suppose it is better for him
And then the doorbell rang.

We all, my mum, my dad and me,
Ran to the door,
We all knew who it was.

And then it all happened so quickly,
My dad sat, just staring, not moving,
My mum and me just stood together.

He was gone, just one quick shot.

Rowan Le Sage (14)
Thomas Keble School, Stroud

The Lingering Lion

A lion, struts in the wild,
A lion no man can tame;
He stands before his prey, mild,
Sick of this game.

But he stares, with submissive eyes,
At a piece of forgotten food,
As if he meant to testify,
A sense of gratitude.

Once again he dwells in the waste,
Shoulders stark and jaws grim,
Licking his lips as he digests the taste,
An intelligent child will not play with him.

Kayleigh MacGillivray (15)
Thomas Keble School, Stroud

The Pond

My gramp cleanly slicing
An inch think clay
And building a wall in the wheelbarrow
And glancing over to watch me play.

I'd come and go collecting
And giving tools to my dad
Who was helping my gramp,
But I looked up to my gramp more that day.

After the pond lining was in,
We left a hose dangling into the black hole
Slowly filling it, like slow rising flood water
Leaving any small bug left in its peril.

Now life's moved on the pond has been
Overrun by wildlife
And my gramp has gone
But that pond will always remind me.

Harry Wilkins (15)
Thomas Keble School, Stroud

Myth

Bizarre creatures of Greek mythology,
Strange beings that only the mind can see.
A woman cursed by gods with snakes for hair,
Petrifies anyone with one cold glare.
An evil king's son, human with bull's gaze,
A ferocious killer, trapped in a maze.
Capable of tearing people into shreds,
A fearsome guardian bearing three heads.
One horrific beast with more heads than three,
The dragon that terrorises the sea.
The large one-eyed behemoth void of wit,
Powerful in strength and rocks it can split.
If you see any of these you should flee,
But they are legendary history.

Joe Jenkins (14)
Thomas Keble School, Stroud

First Day At School

We stopped in the car
I wanted to stay in there
At quarter to nine the bell rang
We walked to the entrance.

At the entrance, I met other kids
Standing, clinging onto their mothers
Like a baby kangaroo in its mother's pouch
The headmaster came out to meet us.

He showed us to our teacher and room
There she was, smiling at our mums
At last, our parents had left us
Our teacher read the register.

It was silent and no one knew
What we had to say, even though
She had told us, she called my name,
My heart stopped, I froze and I had butterflies.

I said, 'Yes, Miss,' and she eventually
Ended the register and we all had to
Say something about us
We only said about four words.

I didn't say a lot, I was frightened
It had been the longest I'd been away from my parents
I wanted to leave.

Tom Pugh (14)
Thomas Keble School, Stroud

Shark

S wift swimmer
H erring destroyer
A lways alert
R azor teeth
K ing fisher.

Max Freedman (11)
Thomas Keble School, Stroud

Childhood Memory

I sat all morning in the sitting room
Counting the minutes till 10 o'clock
Waiting for my friend to ring
So I could go round.

Ring, ring! The phone rings
I answer, it's my friend
She tells me to go round there
They are having a bonfire.

I go round and her mum answers the door
She says they are at the bottom of the garden
And that I should go down.

I go down, down, down
I could smell the bonfire smell
I knew my clothes would smell of it the next day
They come into sight and I stop to wave
They wave back and I carry on running.

I run and then . . .
I trip
I stumble
I fall
Straight into the bonfire.

I get up not feeling any pain
Thinking that I might have missed it
I look down and my knees are covered in ash
I brush off the ash and my knees kill!

My friend goes to get her mum, who rings my mum
By the time my mum gets there, my knees are being bathed
I go to hospital and they bandage my legs up.

Lauren Bown (14)
Thomas Keble School, Stroud

Remember Me!

Leaving for the silent land, remember,
I wish I left before this December,
Please can you remember me now mother,
Please tell my message to my poor brother,
Please do not forget me, only my sins,
Leave my very few things to my next of kin.
Remember, remember, remember me,
Feel good to laugh at your afternoon tea,
Although I am gone, I won't forget you.
Only the bad sins of my aunty Sue.
Where I am, I will always love you all,
But if my friends call for me, tell them that . . .
Leaving for the silent land, remember,
I wish I left before this December.

Amanda Gapp (13)
Thomas Keble School, Stroud

Remember Me

I'm still here do not fear
I will always stand near
I am the fluffy dice in your car
I am your favourite football
I may be dead
But do not cry
Because I am all around you
I am the seam on your favourite cricket ball
Your favourite bat
I will always stand by you
If you stand by me
I may be dead in body
But alive in all of your hearts.

Sam Assanakis (13)
Thomas Keble School, Stroud

Remember Me!

Remember the good days not the bad ones
Remember the way we used to laugh
Look at the pictures we were so happy
Look at the trophies which Dad always won
You will follow your future's long path
You will not cry but find a young chappie
Forget the bad times, remember the good
Forget the arguments, we didn't mean it
Celebrate the life I had now I'm gone
Celebrate the way I spent with you
Get on with your life that is what you should
Get away from going down in the pits
We were so great together it lasted so long
We would have got on with life, you should too.

Corrie-Beth Hill (14)
Thomas Keble School, Stroud

Remember Me!

Remember me as really *loud*
The bubbly kind of chick
I am not mean or really proud
Unless they get on my wick
To other people I don't know
I may be a little shy
But I know I should give it a go
And that's how I get by
I love my sport it's so cool
I'd do it every day you know
Netball, rounders, even football
Well, that's *Jade* for ya!

Jade Shelton (13)
Thomas Keble School, Stroud

God's World

'Come into my world'
'Come into my world'
A voice from the shadows called
Tap, tap, footsteps sound into the bright world
Tears of sorrow dry to smiles of joy
Lurking dark shadows turn to guidance of an angel
Hatred, fear vanquished
Transformed to glittering sparkles of love and hope
Damp, dark weeds embellished into roses
Springing light to the world
A man, tall and peaceful circles from the puffy white clouds
He stares entranced into the undisturbed pond
Light reflects on his pale face
Visions of smiling people fill the water
They were speaking his name
His rose-coloured lips curved and his blue eyes twinkled
And he lived peacefully in God's world forever.

Victoria Butcher (11)
Westonbirt School, Tetbury

Sadness

Sadness is the sound of screaming and crying
Sadness feels like an eruption inside you
Sadness tastes of bitter black charcoal
Sadness smells of hot scorching lava
Sadness looks like a cold winter's day
Sadness reminds me of my granny who has passed away.

Alexia Kyriazi (11)
Westonbirt School, Tetbury

My Little Sister, Lis

My little sister Lis is very sweet,
She likes to eat a lot of sweets.
She tells me she wants to be a sweet one day
And be the best sweet in the world,
Says my little sister, Lis.

My little sister Lis like to ride,
She tells me she wants to be a jockey . . .
She wants to win the Grand National,
On her little pony, Edwyn,
Says my little sister, Lis.

My little sister Lis can be a silly billy
And she tells me not to be silly,
Nevertheless, I do not mind,
I think it is funny,
I love my little sister, Lis!

Georgina Lee (13)
Westonbirt School, Tetbury